voices of
HOME**PARK**

voices of
HOMEPARK

John Lloyd

TEMPUS

Frontispiece: An aerial view of the old Home Park, origin unknown.

First published 2003

Tempus Publishing Limited
The Mill, Brimscombe Port,
Stroud, Gloucestershire, GL5 2QG

© John Lloyd, 2003

The right of John Lloyd to be identified as the Author
of this work has been asserted by him in accordance with the
Copyrights, Designs and Patents Act 1988.

British Library Cataloguing in Publication Data.
A catalogue record for this book is available from the British Library.

ISBN 0 7524 2949 3

Typesetting and origination by Tempus Publishing Limited
Printed in Great Britain by Midway Colour Print, Wiltshire

Contents

Acknowledgements

Putting this book together has been a fantastic experience for me. Reading the submissions from a hundred different contributors has taken me back through Argyle's long history, well beyond my own time as a fan. Some of the stories you are about to read are inspiring, some are sad, some are hilarious, and some are downright bizarre! But there is a common thread running through all of them – an overwhelming sense of belonging, of community, and of shared experience that exists amongst Argyle fans.

The stories in this book are genuine memoirs from Argyle fans of all ages and backgrounds. Some are from veterans who started watching Argyle before the Second World War, while others are from newer fans who have been drawn to Home Park by the recent success of Paul Sturrock's Championship side. What is clear to me is that there are thousands more stories like these yet to be told. Perhaps we will do them justice in a future edition of this book.

In the meantime, there are many people I need to thank for their invaluable assistance in the production of this book. First, and foremost, are the dozens of Argyle fans who took the time to write their stories down and send them in; James Howarth and Becky Gadd at Tempus Publishing, both Argyle fans themselves, for their encouragement, advice and support during the editing and production process; Gordon Sparks, the 'Voice of Argyle', who started the ball rolling in the first place; Dave Rowntree, for kindly supplying so many great pictures; Paul Roberts, Keith Whitfield, Tim O'Hare, Peter Jones and John Coker for casting their eyes over the initial drafts and making some great suggestions; Trevor Scallan for checking some of the facts and figures with the aid of his amazing website (www.geocities.com/pilgrimtrev); Dawn Walsh at QD Computers of Ivybridge; Steve Dean at Greens on Screen (www.greensonscreen.com); Rick Cowdery; Dave Gadd, Steve Barrie and all at PASOTI (www.argyle.org.uk); and Steve Hill. I hope I haven't forgotten anybody!

Enjoy the book and know that by buying it, you have made an important contribution to the Plymouth Argyle Supporters Training and Development Trust, which is dedicated to supporting the Youth of Argyle. To learn more about the work of the Trust, visit www.argyletrust.org.uk. By reading about the past, you have contributed to the future.

John Lloyd,
July 2003

Forewords

Being a supporter of Plymouth Argyle is not something you choose to do when taking an interest in football. You either are, or you aren't. Loyalty is not measured by staying a few seasons with a supposed 'top club' – the club one could have supported since they won the FA Cup or the Premiership. To follow the Pilgrims is a natural thing. Maybe it's because you are a Plymothian, or it's a family tradition. To me, it's both.

My father took me to reserve matches as soon as I could walk. He was a leading light in the Vice-Presidents' Club and secretary of the Shareholders' Association for many years. He would walk to Home Park to renew his and Mum's season ticket on the day the renewal letter landed on the doormat. It was not that he thought his regular seat in the Grandstand might be snapped up in a season ticket sell-out, but the anticipation that he could be buying the tickets to a promotion season.

Like every other Argyle fan, he had to endure the lows. Too many to count. There were also occasional great days and memorable nights. Perhaps that's the great thing about supporting Argyle. Expect the unexpected. Milk every ounce of the good times, like trips to Villa Park, Wembley, and the Lord Mayor's parlour. Enjoy the performances of Johnny Hore, Paul Mariner, Kevin Hodges and Tommy Tynan.

For some fans, the memories fade. I, for one, can't remember the last time that we were defeated by some team in red and white up the road. Can you? I bet you can recall that late winner in the last game in East Devon. Hopefully, on reading those lines, the true feeling of being an Argyle fan is felt within. Great, isn't it? Try explaining that to a fan that travels for four hours to go to a 'home' game in Manchester for no obvious reason. This is football. Real football. Give me a pasty in a paper bag rather than a prawn sandwich any day.

Gordon Sparks

Many of our experiences get lost in the passage of time and to have a book which records those experiences for all time will be invaluable. The only problem for me is a lot of my older experiences are difficult to recall (due to old age, I would add) and with the wonderful experiences of the 2001/2002 Championship-winning season fresh in my mind, it is not surprising. Paul Sturrock has done a wonderful job here and long may it continue. We all are on an upward curve and if we continue to pull together, nothing is impossible. Well done to John in putting this great book together. Forever Green.

Paul Stapleton (chairman, PAFC)

What an honour it is to be contributing to this book. Being an Argyle fan is something special. It's part of our DNA and a large part of our lives. The club's a real anchor-point for us all; whatever we do and wherever we go, we always come back to Home Park.

My memory-banks are absolutely full of Argyle stuff. The *Desert Island* list (in no logical order): Summers scoring to beat Portsmouth 1-0 back in April '87; watching the famous Johnny Newman/Mike Trebilcock penalty way back when; Paul Williams' goal against Colchester in the play-off semi-final; seeing Mariner for the first time; the trip back from Darlington in '02; Bristol City in '86; Hodges' chance at Villa Park; Alan Miller's wonderful save from Oldham's Andy Ritchie in Ken Brown's time. Problem is, of course, the list changes all the time!

All credit to John Lloyd, and to the ninety-odd contributors. It's a great read, it's in a good cause, and it's all about Argyle. What could possibly be better?!

Peter Jones (vice-chairman, PAFC)

From the day my father introduced me to Home Park, I was hooked. There's nowhere like it, anywhere in the world – and there's no club like Argyle. The team of the Thirties was wonderful to watch. It included Sammy Black, about whom I talk later in this book. He was, quite simply, the best Argyle player I ever saw. A fast and skilful winger, his best trick was to cut in from the left and hit an unerringly accurate shot into the corner of the net – all along the ground.

We've had many great moments since. In recent years, the day we won by a single goal at Portsmouth, with just a handful of matches still to play, is still vivid in my memory. We travelled back convinced that that we were about to make the step up to the top division. Many public houses were witness to our unshakeable belief!

We're still waiting for what Plymouth deserves – a team representing the city in the top flight of football. But the great news is that we now have in Paul Sturrock the man I believe will go down in history as our best ever manager. This is a fascinating book. I look forward with great anticipation to its second edition, revised to incorporate two more promotions – with no relegation before, after, or even sandwiched in between.

Rt Hon. Michael Foot

A word from the manager

Football is often about the 'Glory Days' – those wonderful times when something very special happens. Last season's final match at Home Park, followed by the Championship presentations, was one such an occasion. It was truly a magic day, one that few players, fans or managers enjoy throughout their careers and lives.

The scenes on that day will be an abiding memory for me, particularly the crowds outside the Civic Centre in Plymouth and those who lined the route of the open-top bus tour the following Sunday.

My other main memories from an extraordinary season came on our travels, particularly the night we won promotion at Rochdale and the night we claimed the Championship at Darlington. The away fans were tremendous throughout each game and afterwards with their 'on the pitch' celebrations.

One thing that has amazed me in the relatively short time I have been at Home Park has been the away support, especially impressive for a team in such a remote part of the country. We have a remarkable following from fans based around the nation, but the numbers that travel from the depths of the south-west, added to the numbers who travel down from all points north and east for the home matches, never fails to astound me.

The Argyle fans deserve, and receive, my praise, plus that of all the coaching staff and the players. It is the fans that ultimately provide my memories. I just hope I can continue to add to theirs.

Paul Sturrock (manager, PAFC)

The first of many champagne celebrations for 2001/02 takes place in the away dressing room at Spotland, as the Pilgrims make sure of promotion (at least) from Division Three.

1 First match

I became interested in Argyle from the age of 17, but living in Turnchapel, Home Park was a very long way away, requiring a trip across the Cattewater by ferry to Phoenix Wharf. My father was a Centre Stand season-ticket holder, and he promised to take me with him one day. I could hardly wait, and the great day came on Easter Saturday, 1922, when Argyle were at home to Southampton in the old Third Division (South). Argyle won 1-0, and the scorer from the inside-right position (no 4-4-2 nonsense in those days!) was Tommy Gallogley. Unfortunately, Argyle missed promotion that year, although Southampton were promoted. At this match, as with others in the early 1920s, at the half-time whistle, two or three pigeons flew out with the score attached to their legs, presumably destined for distant newspaper offices!

Harold Pascho

I am now 83 years of age and still wouldn't miss an Argyle match for all the tea in China. The first game I attended at Home Park was on Good Friday, 1930. In those days, clubs played three matches in four days at Easter. That year was Argyle's first promotion season. They beat Newport County 3-1 on Good Friday, and Norwich City 4-1 on Easter Saturday. On Easter Monday, they beat Newport County, 2-0

away in the return match, to clinch promotion. My lasting memory of the Norwich game was Jack Vidler being carried off in the first half with concussion. Sure enough, Argyle came out for the second half with ten men (no subs in those days). Then about ten minutes later, Jack Vidler emerged from the tunnel with his head heavily bandaged, and he proceeded to score two more goals to complete his hat-trick. It was said afterwards that he didn't remember a thing about it! This must have whetted my appetite because I have been an Argyle fanatic ever since.

Norman Adams

I have supported Argyle since 1932 when I was 5 years old. My first game was a reserve match against Torquay, with Bill Harper in the Argyle goal, one of the nicest people I have ever met.

Peter Hall

My granddad used to work every Saturday morning, come home to have some lunch and then go off to the match – first team one week, reserves the next. I had been to a reserve match some time before he took me to a first-team game, but I think they used to only get about 10,000 for reserves, whilst the first team got about two or three times that number. I used to really look forward to getting my Teddy Weekes sweets in a little triangular paper bag on the way in and then standing on a small folding stool next to my granddad as we watched. Granddad took me to my first Argyle game way back in the 1938/39 season, and I have on several occasions tried to find out who we played. All I remember is that it was a team playing in white shirts, and that I was frightened out of my wits when I was passed from back on the terraces down to the front, with lots of other small boys who were also passed down in the same way, so that we could see – but I could not even see granddad! It was a nice touch, which is never seen today, as far as I know.

Ken Jones

Picture the scene. The ground is packed, Argyle having won 2-0 against a team who had played like bad-tempered Argentinians, especially late in the second half, and the Grandstand patrons were, amazingly, throwing their hired cushions out onto the pitch at the end of the game! Even to a 12-year-old with very little interest in Argyle at that time, it was obviously a crucial match for both clubs, and the fact that Argyle won triggered the cushions incident. For that reason, the memory stayed with me for many years, until I developed my present-day historical interest in Argyle, and I just had to find out which game I had watched and why there had been such a crazy reaction from the spectators in the stand. From consulting my collection of Argyle handbooks, I managed to identify the game as the last match of the 1954/55 season, which had been played against

Stoke City on 30 April. From further research, I discovered that Argyle had been in a relegation battle with Ipswich Town, who had only been promoted from the Third Division (South) the previous season. Just for good measure, Stoke had been one of five clubs contesting the two promotion places, there being no play-offs at that time. Derby County had already been relegated in 22nd (last) position, and Argyle were one point ahead of Ipswich with a slightly better goal average, but to be absolutely sure of avoiding the drop, they had to win their last game of the season, as did Stoke to stand a chance of going up from their position in 2nd place. Ipswich were away at Notts County, who had been on the fringe of the promotion place, but were no longer in contention. Thanks to a George Willis goal, Argyle were 1-0 to the good at half-time, and there was a tense five minutes or so to wait before the crowd were made aware of the other relevant half-time scores. In those days, you needed a programme, or at least a mate who had one, to find them out, as they were not announced over the loudspeakers as they are today. Each game was allocated a letter of the alphabet, all of which were displayed on the Popular Side fence, on the front of the old director's box (now the Chisholm Lounge), and at the corner of the Barn Park End and the Grandstand, with the programme revealing the match allocated to each letter. Because of this, programme sales must have been higher than normal at this game, the attendance being just below 24,000. The half-time scores also revealed that only one of Stoke's rivals were winning, and both teams must have been aware of this when they took the field for the second half. When Argyle scored their second through Hugh McJarrow,

Stoke lost their self-control. If the game had been played today, more than a few red cards would have been handed out, not to mention numerous arrests of the stand patrons! As it happened, Ipswich Town lost 1-2 at Meadow Lane, and Argyle were safe in any case, but the Home Park crowd were unaware of this, and the sense of relief must have been tremendous, hence the spontaneous reaction. At that time, the only way of finding out other full-time scores was to get home in time to tune into *Sports Report* on the radio at five o'clock, or wait for the *Football Herald* to be delivered. There was no television coverage and, indeed, very few people had a set in any case. With the other results that day, Stoke would have needed to beat Argyle 5-0 to have gone up, but they took some revenge six seasons later when they inflicted Argyle's record 0-9 defeat. Unfortunately, Argyle only delayed the inevitable that day, as they were relegated the following season.

Phil Hollow

It was back on Saturday 30 August 1958. I was just 4 and went along with my Dad. Argyle were playing Tranmere, I was on the edge of the Spion Kop and could only see around the sides of the people there until I was lifted on top of the fence. When the teams came out onto the field and over 22,000 cheered, I was a bit scared. When Argyle scored the first of their goals, I was hooked. The fact Argyle won 4-0 did not really matter. From that day, I wanted more of the same and have been an Argyle supporter since.

Keef Newham

I can't remember the exact first match. My father worked for the Supporters' Club, which was then Argyle's commercial arm. He used to sell scarves, rosettes and things called golliwogs (this was the 1950s) in a hut at the back of the Barn Park End. The first match that I can remember in any detail is the 5-1 defeat by Spurs in the FA Cup. There was a capacity crowd of 40,000, and the best team in the land playing Argyle. Great atmosphere, bad result.

Keith Whitfield

I was first taken to Home Park in the late Sixties by my godfather, Uncle Fred. He was a St John's Ambulance volunteer and when I was lucky enough to go, I got to sit on a wooden bench on the cinder track, right next to the pitch on the Mayflower side, equidistant from the halfway line and the Barn Park End. Unfortunately, I don't remember the actual first game, but my earliest memory is of the Boxing Day game against Torquay in 1969. Norman Piper, who wore the number 6 on his shirt, was firmly established as my favourite player by this time and when the Argyle crowd started to chant, 'WE WANT SIX', I was filled with a really warm feeling of togetherness. I was part of a huge number of people and we all loved Norman. I leaned over and told my uncle this. He kindly said, 'Err, not exactly son, we're winning 5-0 and everyone wants us to get a sixth!' (Which, of course, Argyle did).

Jan Walaszkowski

My first match was at the start of the 1959/60 season, with Argyle newly in the

Second Division. The visitors were Sheffield United, who scored first. Their 'keeper was Alan Hodgkinson, a recent England international, and I thought we would never score until up stepped Johnny Williams (Williams, J.S. in the programme), who let go a screamer from thirty yards out and became my favourite player for a long time to come. That first season back, Argyle struggled, although their home form was not bad. The last match of the season we entertained Aston Villa, already promoted to the First Division, and with a side comprising several internationals, whose photos appeared in all the soccer mags. They had players such as Peter MacParland, Gerry Hitchens and Pat Saward. Argyle formed a guard of honour and clapped them onto the pitch. From then on, Argyle dominated and won 3-0. George Kirby nearly did a Beckham (before Beckham was born) and hit the crossbar from the halfway line.

Kevin Howarth

May 1969 and my dad – who was in the Navy – was posted to Plymouth. As an 11-year-old, how disappointed I was that we were returning to UK to a place that had 'a crappy Third Division team'. Before we went to Malta in December 1966, we had lived in Southampton – newly promoted to the First Division – for a few short months after England's World Cup success. I had spent the first half of 1966/67 season watching the likes of Bobby Charlton, Geoff Hurst and Bobby Moore representing their clubs at the Dell. I suspect that if we had not moved halfway through the season, I would now be a Saints fan. However, I got into Maltese football –

Floriana in particular, who also play in green and white – before arriving in Plymouth at the end of 1968/69. I was by now hooked on football and needed a regular 'fix'. Argyle were the only team locally, so my dad and I headed for Home Park for the first time on the evening of Wednesday 13 August to watch a League Cup tie with Torquay. Our visitors were also in the Third Division. We were held to a 2-2 draw in front of a crowd of over 15,000. All I remember is that we stood by the fence at the corner between the Devonport End and Mayflower Terrace in what is now the Family Enclosure. We lost the replay 1-0 a week later in front of over 10,000 at Plainmoor and, three days later, we won the League game at Plainmoor 2-1 with nearly 11,000 in the ground. On Boxing Day that season, we beat Torquay 6-0 in front of over 17,000 at Home Park.

Steve Nicholson

My first match was sometime in 1975, when I was in my early teens. My friend thought we should go to Argyle in the hope of meeting some boys. I can't remember who we were playing, but that was my first sight of Mariner and Rafferty. I fell in love with the game, and with Argyle, and it's lasted ever since. PS – Needless to say, we didn't meet any boys!

Peggy Prior

FA Cup third round v. Blackpool, January 1975. My dad made a special effort to go to this one – he liked the Cup – and I tagged along. We stood on the Spion Kop, right near the front, and watched mesmerised as Billy Rafferty scored twice to win the tie and set up a next round match against Everton. It was the Tony Waiters promotion season, so it was easy to keep on going, and, of course, once you're hooked there's no going back. Incidentally, I never ever stood on the Spion corner again, until I sat in the new stand against Swindon at Christmas 2002.

Steve Barrie

The first match for me was on Tuesday 4 April 1978 at home against Sheffield Wednesday, the day I became hooked. The score was 1-1 and the attendance was 7,694. I can't remember much, except that it was probably the only time I ever stood in the Devonport End, and my Auntie Jane, who took me, fancied the 'keeper (was it Ramsbottom?). The preferred viewpoint thereafter became the corner between the Lyndhurst and Devonport (just underneath the pylon).

Chris Ramsay

28 July 1979, Argyle *v.* Newcastle – a friendly that we lost 3-0. My memories were of Kevin Keegan scoring (later research showed it was Peter Withe – similar barnets caused the problem, I think); going to a match with my dad and both my grandfathers for what turned out to be the

Billy Rafferty formed a lethal striking partnership with Paul Mariner.

only time; drinking Bovril for the first time; and the dirty looks from those around me on the Lyndhurst when I exposed my Argyle shirt (people didn't seem to wear shirts much then). Feeling self-conscious, I put my parka back on and didn't wear a shirt to a football match for another eight years!

Richard Smith

22 April 1980 *v.* Southend. This was back in the days of Sims, Kemp and co. I don't really remember too much about the game. It was a hot April day, there must have been a crowd of about 5,500 and I stood in the Devonport End behind the goal with my mate Mike. There were few chances and it was the last home game of the season. I remember shots by John Sims and a few efforts from Kempy (who was a little off-form that day). Southend didn't put up too much of a game either, so it was pretty drab end-of-season stuff. We were a mid-table team going nowhere, with nothing to play for but pride. But the atmosphere in the Devonport End was good, the pasties were good (no peas in them) and it was my first live game ... followed by my first full season in 1980/81 and the introduction of Donal Murphy, one of Argyle's finest wingers.

Andy Laidlaw

I can remember the match, but not who it was. We lost 1-0, but the home crowd for that game stood in the Barn Park End. My dad said to me 'that was rubbish, wasn't it?' but I just thought the whole thing was brilliant! Hooked ever since!

Dave Gadd

6 December 1980 *v.* Rotherham, we won 3-1 at home. My dad is a Rotherham fan, so I guess if the result had been different that day, the last twenty-plus years of my life might have been different and I might now support a First Division side. Nothing particularly interesting happened, although we did miss the first half because Dad had left his money at home and he had to find a mate to borrow some off. Bleddy tight Yorkshiremen ... My sister's first game was somewhat more notable; she was visiting me at university and I had arranged for her to go shopping with my girlfriend. However, she insisted on coming to the football, although in hindsight, she maintains that it would have been cheaper to have gone to the Metro Centre. The game? 7 May 1994, away *v.* Hartlepool, 8-1!

Mark Colling

I commenced my love affair with The Greens in 1984. I think everybody remembers his or her first visit to Home Park. As a small child, I trundled my way across Central Park, the lights getting nearer, the chants getting louder. I witnessed a multitude of grown-ups walking with a sense of purpose and eagerness, walking religiously to a Mecca-like glow in the distance. The nickname 'The Pilgrims' had never appeared more appropriate! I can vividly remember walking to the ground with a sense of anticipation and bewilderment. Upon entering this cauldron of green and white, I took my place in the Lyndhurst Stand and observed in uncertainty. Why was everybody eating pasties? Why were our supporters so malicious to theirs? Their goalkeeper wasn't that fat, surely? To my left, in the Barn Park End, a scattering of

Lincoln fans. The true devotion of such supporters still remains an inspiration, following their team through good and bad, in fair weather and foul. To my right, the throaty Devonian burr of the Devonport End, awash with adoring support. Opposite, the almost paternal expectancy of the Grandstand looked down on us. I knew that I was addicted. My first jersey was conscientiously bought soon after, and, like in a romantic novel, the relationship commenced. My school years bordered upon obsession. I would arrive an hour before kick-off for reserve games to monitor the form of up-and-coming players. I knew the League positions Argyle had finished in pre-war off by heart. Why did I know this? Why did I want to know this? Why could I recount effortlessly the names of the players' girlfriends or wives, yet have such difficulty remembering uncomplicated mathematical concepts at school? Fascination was clearly turning into mania, such was my devotion. If Argyle had been a girl, I would have been arrested for stalking. Every Saturday involved the same dedicated routine, seeing the same passionate characters, week in, week out, for our weekly dose of tribal feuding. The memories seem so lucid even now – the 1-1 draw with Everton in the FA Cup, seeing mates cry with happiness after Mickey Evans scored for us in the 96th minute against Barnet on a cold Tuesday night, the mighty highs of the play-offs in 1996, coupled with the suicidal despondency of the Burnley game. If only … Fortunately, the anticipation, expectancy and naïve optimism still remain. They will be there for many seasons to come. Anything else would be infidelity.

Julian Burrows

My first match was versus Hull City in 1987. We won 3-1, thanks to goals from Mark Smith, John Clayton and Tommy Tynan. I remember seeing the Leeds game highlights on TV and asking my dad if we could go up to see Argyle play. Due to my dad working for Barclays (the League sponsors at the time), he sorted out some tickets for the Grandstand and the rest, as they say, is history.

Benjie Ward

22 October 1991, Argyle 4 Millwall 0 in the ZDS Cup. I think it was a Tuesday night. The ground was pretty empty – well, as empty as it can be with a 2,000 crowd – but I remember thinking that the noise in the Lyndhurst was amazing. To cap it all, we hammered them! I got hooked and, by the end of the season, was one of the many shedding tears when we went down against Blackburn.

Joe Fielder

Argyle *v.* Brentford, 6 November 1993, aged 9. Dalton scored for us, and Joe Allon got theirs. Being young and enthusiastic, I remember even filling in the bit on the back of the programme counting how many corners each side got – it was something like 20-1 in Argyle's favour! If only the final score was that way. However, they were the only goals I saw at Home Park for the next six matches or so – I think I must have managed to see every 0-0 that Argyle played at home for the next few seasons!

James Pender

March '96 v. Gillingham, we won 1-0. I had never really thought about going to watch Argyle, but my dad arranged to take me up one Saturday. We stood in the Family Stand and I was just amazed. I didn't sing or shout, just watched the game in silence. When Martin Barlow scored the goal from about 8 yards on a slight angle across the goal (I can still see it now), the noise from the Devonport was like nothing I had ever heard before. I didn't realise at the time that beating Gillingham was important for promotion. When I got home, I looked up the League on the TV and there we were, right near the top. Then, I watched out for the results every week, pestering my Dad to take me again, especially to Wembley. Unfortunately, we didn't go again until the next season, but after that first game, I was addicted.

Rob Wallbank

I had been on holiday with my dad and family in Portugal and we had missed the first two home matches. I was six years old and Dad had promised to buy me a season ticket and take me to the football. When we got home, Dad had withdrawal symptoms and decided to take me to Ashton Gate to watch us play against Bristol City. It was a good crowd, a dry day and I watched intently, trying to understand the rules, and listening to the singing – who was the 'Banker' in the black? Well, those were the words my dad told me were being sung. What was offside? It didn't matter, Dad said the linesmen didn't know either. We drew 1-1, Andy Thomas scored a penalty. Dad knew Rhys Wilmot, our goalie, and he told me he got booked at half-time for arguing with the referee. Never answer back, he told me. I had sweets, an Oxo drink and a pie (no pasties), so I had a good day. 'Did you enjoy it?' my Dad asked me on the way back down the A38 to Plymouth. Yes I did, I said hesitantly, but do we have to come so far every week? I didn't know why my dad laughed all the way home. Memories eh?

Oliver Stapleton

2 Where do you watch matches from?

The Devonport End. My first match was there. The atmosphere was there when I was an impressionable youth. When I learnt the game, as a player and a watcher, I believed the behind-the-goal view was the best from which to see the play and tactics unfold – and still do.

Malcolm Sheryn

I guess I have been fairly migratory in my Argyle watching. My first vantage point was at the site of the old Family Stand in the corner between the old Devonport End and Mayflower Terrace. In those early days, I used to change ends depending which way Argyle were attacking, as did many others. At that time, you could even get into the Barn Park (Zoo) End, but that was stopped sometime in the Seventies. I started going regularly with my friends into the Devonport End in the early Seventies. We stayed as close as we dared to the big boys who were doing all the singing. Eventually, we even became big enough to be part of the gang in the all-singing/all-dancing Devonport End. When the Devonport End roof was removed for safety reasons, most of the regulars there – including me – migrated to the Barn Park End of the Lyndhurst – which was standing only in those days. I discovered that the terracing was better than in the

Devonport, and the overall view of the match much improved, so even when the Devonport roof was replaced, I stayed put. When the seats were installed in the Lyndhurst, I was unhappy. I did not want to sit down to watch my football. I tried it, but could not settle. I went back to the Devonport, but missed the side-on view of the match. This is when I became a regular on the Mayflower terrace. I have been there ever since – until the season when the redevelopment began. With the rebuilding work going on, I was forced to reconsider my vantage point, as the Mayflower's days were numbered. I did see some of the 2001/02 season from the Mayflower Terrace, but selling fanzines until five to three and with so many people crammed into so little space, a decent view was impossible. I tried the Main Stand before Christmas that season and various points along the new Lyndhurst once the building was completed. I have now returned to the Lyndhurst permanently. As I get older, sitting down is becoming the preferable option anyway!

Steve Nicholson

I suspect that, with the vast majority of fans, they are fixtures. By pure chance, possibly, they came to their first match at Home Park and rather like attending a conference or seminar, on re-entering the room (in this case, the ground), they adopt the same seat or position as they did last time. This then builds up into a habit or ritual for several reasons. Firstly, they acquire an 'I belong here' mentality. Secondly, they form an acknowledging nod-of-head relationship with others who sit or stand in that particular area, to the point that one gets on a conversational level with complete strangers, and the individual becomes a Lyndhurster, or a Devonport Ender, or indeed, a Mayflower Terracer. If you are rich and have no nerve endings in your rear end, then one becomes a wooden-seated Grandstander! Occasionally, one might change their allegiance. Having started life as a Greenie positioned right under the announcer's window, it was quite soon that I graduated to become a Devonport Ender and spent many seasons stood on exactly the same piece of covered terrace. It became mine almost to the extent that others knew their place and by mutual consent and respect, no one encroached onto another's domain. This rather went out of the window for large attraction matches, and I recall the affront felt when some hairy Man Utd fan had the temerity to park himself on my bit of terrace, simply because they were playing St Etienne at Home Park! Allegiance then swung towards the covered Lyndhurst when the roof came off the Devonport, and considerable fun was experienced when lumps of rust fell off into one's half-time tea – such was the state of the Lyndhurst covering. In fact, few fans ever realised that they were stood over a fox den which was housed under their feet! It was from my vantage point in the Lyndhurst at one fixture with a healthy crowd, that I saw a small terrier dog break

free from its master and hare across the pitch. With typical Argyle fans' responsive humour, the cry instantly went up – 'One Jack Russell, there's only one Jackie Russell, one Jackie Russell, there's only one Jackie Russell'. The dog was quite nippy, so this instant retort was followed by the more traditional 'Sign him on, sign him on, sign him on!'. Seating is not my preferred way to watch football – so when the original plastic was introduced on that side, divorce swiftly followed, and I allowed myself to become involved with the remaining standing area – the Mayflower Terrace. This had some advantages. It is still accessible just before kick-off to those who wish to utilise the Far Post Club. If you stand at the back, you get an excellent elevation and view – and the overhanging Grandstand affords shelter from the South-Westerlies. Nor do you have the setting sun burning into your head at those late summer and spring games. It's probably the more vocally restrained of the three Argyle sides as far as noise generated is concerned – unless they feel the referee or opposition are being over-zealous, and then the volume really gets turned up. It's also quite possible to initiate chants from the back of the terrace, which can then be taken up all round the ground. Messrs Kinnear and Co. are also ideally placed for local appreciation societies to express their opinions as to their capabilities or parentage. I know I shouldn't, but there are times when, well, it just has to be said, doesn't it?

Bob Gelder

When my dad first took me to Home Park in the late 1960s, we sat in the Grandstand. We moved away to Helston for a year, but on our return, I started going into the Barn Park (or Zoo) End as it was, especially as school friends did the same. Late teens saw me move into the Devonport, then, as the roof came off, it was the Lyndhurst, where I sort of settled. Once the Lyndhurst became all-seater, I moved over to the other side into the Moan-flower, where I still go – but only because I prefer to watch from the side, and to stand.

Dave Pay

It used to be (circa 1958-1966) dead centre in the Lyndhurst, about three terraces back. However, it was usually nearer the Devonport End to be away from the moron collection at the Barn Park End of the Lyndhurst. My late mother always stood by the tunnel, so she could smell the embrocation! She and my late dad went to matches together, but he stood on what was the Kop. At one time or another, when my brother and sister also went, there was probably a Ramsay in each section of the ground.

John Ramsay

On the Mayflower terraces, by the halfway line. I prefer to stand – it allows circulation to chat with people, and you don't get people standing up in front of you when something exciting happens! It also seems more traditional or natural to stand at football matches. I like the perspective from the halfway line.

Phil Banks

I've always have been a viewer from the very back (except during the enforced Mayflower – shhh! – Terrace exile) in the Lyndhurst and the Devonport (though slightly further over towards the Spion Kop, by the last pillar between the pasty shop and the exit to the bogs). Being at the back, I didn't get my 6ft 6in frame in other people's line of vision and I prefer noisier parts of the ground. Also, you've got something to lean against when things get boring.

Phil Rescorla

When I was a boy, we used to watch Argyle matches from the Spion Kop. Some people maintained that the wooden railway sleepers that made up a lot of the terracing were warmer for your feet than concrete. However, as it was uncovered, it was wetter for your head.

John Haley

I watched a lot of games on the Mayflower Terrace, about four rows back from the front, between the halfway line and the touchline. I would get there early, around 2 p.m., and stake out my spot on one of the barriers. After a break of five years, because I live in the States now, I ended up back at that exact spot when I visited in 2002. It was amazing how the same people were still there, just as I remembered them the last time I was at a game.

Mark Williams

Mayflower seating, row D, just to the Barn Park End of the halfway line. Why? Always

The old Home Park.

Work begins as diggers move in to demolish the Devonport End.

The foundations for the new stadium are prepared.

A new stand starts to take shape.

The new seats are put in.

At last! Phase One of Nou Home Park is complete. The fans enjoy their classy new stadium.

have done. Perhaps I enjoy being surrounded by cynical old farmers from the depths of Cornwall and North Devon.

Tim Anthony

I used to go in the Barn Park End, as a few of us would climb over the fence and get in for nothing (I was only 8 at the time!). Then as I grew up, I moved into the Devonport End, before finally ending up in the new Lyndhurst, as it has a great view.

Terry Adamson

I have always watched from the back of the Dem'port. The views back then weren't as good as they are now, for obvious reasons, but I always have fond memories of the Dem'port, including standing right at the back of the stand, without the roof on it, in the middle of December, freezing my nads off and 'receiving' a football from John Sims – the only man to sky a goalscoring opportunity from 2 yards – when I was but a lad. Ah, memories ...

Andy Laidlaw

I've always watched from the Lyndhurst. When I first went, I sat at the back of the C in the Lyndhurst. It's become home, my place with my friends. None of us would move now and it was the longest six months for us sitting in the Mayflower seating area in the 2001/02 season.

Joe Fielder

I was taken to my first game (in the late Eighties) in the Mayflower by my granddad and have mainly been there with him and other family and friends ever since. Successive poor seasons for Argyle, coupled with moves away from the area, have meant that the number of people I attend with had grown smaller and smaller until midway through the 2001/02 season, when even the old man (a fan since the 1930s) took the somewhat drastic step of moving to South Africa. We were just getting good as well. With no reason to stay in the Mayflower, the novelty value of the shiny new seats, plus the superior atmosphere, persuaded me to frequent the Devonport End more regularly whenever I got the chance to take in a game. Seeing as we've done so well, it'd be tempting fate not to stay there.

Luke Hildyard

I have supported from all parts of the ground. However, for the last twenty-odd years, I have been living in the Devonport End. OK, the view of the game is not so good, but the atmosphere is awesome. It's a sod when we play towards the Devonport in the first half and we can't look forward to the second-half attack at our end. Once you have sampled the Devonport atmosphere, it would take some breaking away from anyway!

Daddy Kool

The Lyndhurst. I saw my first game there in 1986, right in the centre of the terrace, against Derby. Tommy Tynan scored an injury-time equaliser. I went as a Lincoln exile and came away a converted Green. I stayed there even when the seats went in until, coincidentally, the FA Cup game against Derby in '96. I had kids by then, and moved to the Family Stand in the corner. I'm now back in the Lyndhurst, as it is the same price for children regardless of where you sit. A top move by the club.

Paul Whitworth

I started watching Argyle as a 6-year-old from the Grandstand. Once I sat in the next-to-back row, and became aware of someone coming along and sitting in the seat behind me. When I turned around, it was Paul Mariner (long hair and all) who I think had just signed for Argyle, but was yet to make his debut. Still got his autograph some-where. When I was a teenager, I moved to stand at the front of the Mayflower Terrace, near the tunnel, to get players' autographs before the game. Now I always stand near the front of the Mayflower Terrace, roughly in line with the penalty spot nearest the goal Argyle are attacking. I usually change ends so that I'm at the right end to get a good view of our goals going in!

John Simmons

I stand on the Mayflower Terrace, towards the Devonport End. The reasons I go there are tradition, ritual and a sense of belong-ing. It's where I stood when my dad used to take me as a kid. Standing on a terrace is an essential part of the football experi-ence. I like to be close to the match, at pitch level. Sadly, these things won't be true in a few years' time.

Toby Jones

As I have grown up with Argyle, I have moved around the ground. In the 1970s, I stood on the Devonport End. I remember capacity crowds for FA Cup matches (30,000 plus) where the swaying of the crowd caused you to move from one side to another without realising it. Of course, I hardly saw a thing, but singing the old songs generated its own excitement and when Argyle won, you felt that in some way you had contributed. As maturity crept up on me, we moved across to the Lyndhurst Stand. Once seating was installed there, it was off to the Mayflower Terrace to maintain the standing-only tra-dition. However, since Christmas 2001, the only place to be is back on the Lyndhurst in the superb setting that is the new Home Park. Incidentally, I've only sat in the Mayflower Stand once – the Watney Cup match against Stoke City in 1973.

Martin Thomas

I have been going to Argyle for many years, originally with my grandfather, but when I was called up to do my National Service, I never went with him again. A few years later, when my son Adrian was about 5 or 6, we started going with my father-in-law – his grandfather. When my father-in-law passed away, my son and I went together for a long time, until he started going with his pals. But throughout, we always stood in the Devon-port End, behind the Lyndhurst goalpost. Since then, I have stood in the Mayflower, although recently I have been sitting in the Grandstand, having also spent some time there in the past. I don't really think you can beat the Devonport End for atmosphere.

Ken Jones

3 Most significant Argyle matches

Two games stand out for me. The first was the play-off semi-final second leg against Colchester United at Home Park. It was the first time I had watched a game from anywhere other than the middle of the Lyndhurst Stand. I got myself a ticket for the Grandstand to avoid having to turn up hours before kick-off to get a decent seat. I remember the game because the three Argyle goals were almost perfectly timed. Trailing 1-0 from the first leg, Argyle needed an early goal to stamp their authority on the tie – Michael Evans did the business after about 5 minutes. Then, just before half-time, always a good time to score, Chris Leadbitter curled in a free-kick to put Argyle in command. Mark Kinsella scored for Colchester in the second half – an away goal that put them in the driving seat – but then Charlie Williams popped up with just a few minutes to go to plant his magical header into the back of the net. There was no way back for Colchester after that. The second game that had that special something for me was the Boxing Day 2001 game against Cardiff City at Home Park. I don't actually remember much detail, but I do recall that Cardiff had kicked Argyle all around the park, wasted time at every opportunity and generally given the impression that they were oh so superior. Argyle ended up winning 2-1, and I can still feel how I felt when Argyle's second

goal went in (late in the game) and my feeling of elation that Argyle had got their just reward. I leapt up cheering so vigorously that I must have damaged a nerve or something in the back of my head. As I was still in the air, I remember an incredible pain shooting through my head from top to bottom and wondering whether when my feet hit the floor again, the rest of me would keep going and I would end up in a crumpled heap. I didn't, but I'm not convinced my head has ever been the same again.

Tim O'Hare

Preston away in 1997/98. I went with a Preston-supporting mate. I'd only known him a couple of years, but we were close buddies and whoever won would be able to gloat all evening – we've all been there. In the previous season, the fixture had finished 1-1, but we both expected Argyle to get a pasting, what with our usual away form and Preston emerging as a tough team to knock down. After a lot of frights, I was glad to get to half-time still 0-0. I remember thinking this will be a respectable scoreline, even if we lose. In the second half, with 70 minutes gone, Argyle had a rare break, and up popped Carlo Corrazin at the far post with a header to win the game, which provoked some heartfelt celebrations, and I spent the next few minutes trying not to throw up. I remember my mate saying this defeat was on a par with losing a play-off final after being two-up at half-time. He said that he'd never forget my face as I met him outside the Town End. I didn't gloat, but was painfully silent about the whole thing all night – he couldn't look me in the eye, because he knew I was looking straight back going 'aaaahhhhh!' in my mind. The second has to be Rochdale in the 2001/02 Championship season. The second goal was such an anti-climax, but Lee Hodges' third summed up the whole season for me – I still get over-excited when I think about the shot hitting the back of the net. We were always going to get promotion around this point in the season, but the

way we did it against a bloody decent 'Dale team and going one down to an amazing goal. It's a night us Leeds Greens still talk about in the pub. That night was for all the people who have travelled to places like Scarborough on a wet Tuesday night to lose 3-0, Macclesfield 4-1 – actually, this list could go on for a while, but this game made amends for all the crap we've put up with. Everyone who I've come to recognise at away games over the previous seasons in the basement division was there – it was just great. Another of the most memorable games for me would be the Turf Moor play-off semi-final in '94. I'll never forget the tremendous atmosphere and the big flag. The low roof over the Green Army seemed to keep the noise in, and noisy we were. We seemed to be

The Argyle team celebrate their play-off win over Colchester United. Next stop, Wembley.

The Green Army goes wild at Spotland, as promotion from Division Three is secured.

The Argyle fans on the pitch look on as the champagne celebrations begin.

singing for 90 minutes. One of the most battling Argyle displays I've ever seen, coupled with one of the most biased refereeing displays ever seen. The team played with such guts that the home leg could only go one way. This, of course, was followed by one of the worst Argyle displays I've ever seen in the second leg at Home Park, and the rest is history. Some of the most memorable matches for me relate to the disappointment of seeing Argyle lose so much over the years, and so many inept displays. Losing 4-1 in 1997 to Gillingham, when we hoped the fog would stay long enough for the game to be abandoned, but it didn't. Dickov's late winner for Brighton at the Goldstone in 1993/94, and their gloating thereafter. Having that fear every year that we'd be put out in the first round of the FA Cup by Slough or Kingstonian. But the 2001/02 season has put all those demons to bed. Roll on Turf Moor!

Neil Carhart

For me, there are three: Carlisle away (on 13 April 2002), Darlington away (15 April 2002) and Cheltenham Town at home (20 April 2002). I guess, for many that were at all three games, it's something that will stay in their memories for a long time. The sense of camaraderie, friendliness, unity and shared passion was just overwhelming. The complete and utter joy on the faces of fans and players at the end of the Carlisle game, when the result of the Luton match was discovered – everyone knowing that three points at the next match would win the title. The sense of achievement at Darlington when, after going 3-0 up in half-an-hour, everyone

knew that the title was ours. This led to one of the funniest moments I can remember at a football match – the 'Sit down for the Champions' chant! The feeling of future success when the Championship squad was introduced at the Cheltenham game. To see Nou Home Park packed full was a glorious sight, and you just felt that the future of the club was assured.

Chris Prew

The friendliness of the fans at the away clubs where promotion, and then the Championship, in 2001/02 were decided made each game memorable. It was great to see football played in the right spirit, with fans from other clubs appreciating our success and the devotion we had to get to all the games. In order: Rochdale – the anticipation in the lead-up following the glorious day at Sincil Bank (Lincoln) when inflatable champagne bottles first made their appearance. Great spirit in the Church Inn before the game; very few nerves, as we knew promotion was going to happen some time (it was before Easter, for Christ's sake!). Then the game: loads of champagne bottles, including some 6ft monsters. A subdued performance from Argyle, before a fluke goal from the touchline by Paul Simpson. Argyle came to life. The equaliser, the second and then a third to guarantee the three points, let alone the one we needed. The best memory has to be the players diving to celebrate. Unbridled joy amongst everyone when we invaded the pitch. Great stewards allowing us to do the above. The looks on the faces of the players in the 'drektors' box. The long journey home, full of joy. Carlisle: total control, a first-class effort from a team in tangerine for the first time. Seeing fifty or so Dundee United fans there, showing us just how much of a hero our manager was in his playing days up there. Joy at the end. Three points and we'd done it! Darlo: Tap and Spile, great atmosphere beforehand. Expectation, but no feeling of guarantee as at 'Dale. Tangerine (again)! 4-3-3 – pace, movement, incisive passing. 1, 2, 3 – game over, celebrate title. One back by Darlo soon after half-time. Not caring, this was a different team from previous ones which might have collapsed. 4! Unbridled joy. Pitch invasion – policeman asking us to stay off the pitch until the final whistle, not asking us to stay off totally! Players going mental. Darlo fans staying behind (in the main stand and on the pitch) to applaud us, and everyone in the ground (players included) bellowing out 'Are you watching, Joe Kinnear?' Home Park against Cheltenham: trying to get over a very large hangover, knowing a draw would beat the 100-point barrier. Seeing the Cheltenham players doing a guard of honour. Nice touch, and knowing we'd then won the game. Cocko taking care of Julian Alsop (donkey/giraffe cross-breeding experiment) beautifully. 'We are the Champions, no time for Luton, we are the Champions, of the Third!' Then listening to Kinnear gobbing off (again) and laughing every time I heard another snippet of bitterness.

Mark Hope

I can remember absolutely loving Barnet at home in the 1999/2000 season for a variety of reasons. It was the first time I ever went to Home Park with my best mate, who had not previously been a fan,

and who I now attend every match with. It was also the only time I have sat in the Mayflower Grandstand, looking down on everyone else. Although I much prefer my current position at the back of the Devonport, it was nice to have a change. As well as this, Argyle won 4-1 against a side who were at that time second in the League, and they did it with style and flourish. The now not-so-fondly-remembered Paul McGregor was on fire that day, scoring a hat-trick, including a corker from 30 yards. It was one of the only times during the Hodges reign that I really felt we might be going somewhere. Unfortunately, the season came to nothing, but for a few fleeting hours on a cool autumn afternoon, everything was different. I know it's obvious, but my all-time favourite Argyle game was Cheltenham on 20 April 2002 at home and the Championship party. The two-goal victory, the party atmosphere, the trophy presentation, the lap of honour … great days. To quote Paul Wotton the next day: 'We've only gone and done it!!!!'

Richard Partington

Carlisle United 2 Plymouth Argyle 1, 8 May 1999. What happened that day was truly extraordinary, and it wasn't just Jimmy Glass the goalkeeper scoring his injury-time winner. With their Football League survival guaranteed, the Cumbrians, who'd been threatening untold violence moments before, suddenly saw the Argyle fans as their brothers-in-arms. We shook hands, exchanged scarves. I've still got a Carlisle United shirt hanging in the wardrobe, after giving up my Argyle top to one sweaty, happy supporter. The transformation of the

The jubilant players celebrate Argyle's first Championship in over forty years, which was secured in the rearranged match at Feethams.

home support was breathtaking. One minute, they were indicating they'd gladly slit our throats, then we were long-lost best friends. I had never seen anything like it, and I don't think I ever will again. Swansea City 2 Plymouth Argyle 3, 24 April 1999. A truly ridiculous result. At 2-0 down with about twenty minutes to go, I remember looking around at other Argyle fans there and realising that more than half weren't watching the game. They were just chatting amongst themselves. Some were sitting down on the terrace, so they couldn't see anyway. Plenty had their backs to the pitch. But then, amazingly, we came back

from the dead to win 3-2. It was a bit like it happened in slow motion, and every fan in that away terrace just couldn't believe it. Surely one of the most incredible, unlikely turnarounds of all time. I know I'll never forget it.

Sam Fleet

I'm not sure how significant a match it is, but Dave Smith attended this game prior to applying for and being appointed Argyle manager. Having raided my programme drawer, the game was Orient *v.* Argyle in

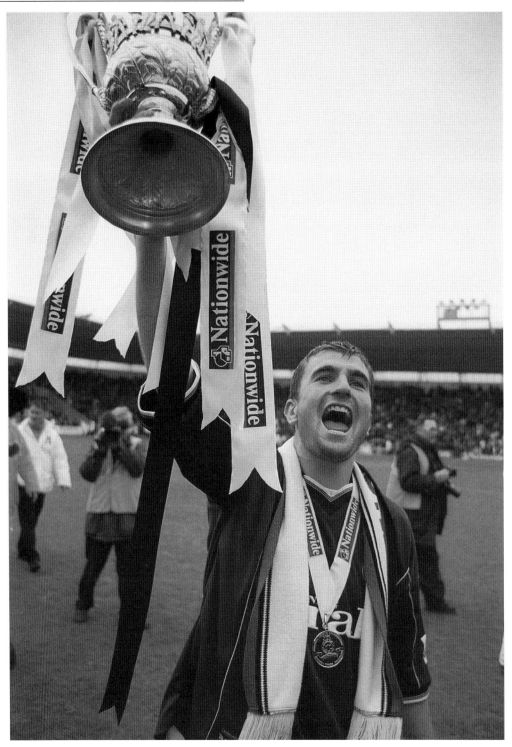

Paul Wotton with the Championship Trophy – 'We've only gone and done it!'

the old Third Division on 23 October 1984. Argyle were managerless at the time. The Orient goalkeeper that game was one Rhys Wilmot, on loan from Arsenal for the season. I used to work and share a house with his sister, who was a close friend of mine, so we got some good tickets to go up and see the game after work. It was a pretty dire display from Argyle and we lost 3-0, the highlight of the game being a stupendous save by Rhys late on in the second half, from what I seem to remember was about Argyle's only shot on target. It was a bizarre moment as I leapt to my feet to celebrate a near certain goal whilst Elizabeth, his sister, leapt to her feet (as did most of the stand) to acknowledge a great save. Apparently, Ciderman attended the game to prepare a dossier on the Argyle team, which he presented at his interview. His comments that the team were 'dispirited' and 'didn't seem to want to play for each other' were spot on. He obviously impressed the board, as he was appointed Argyle manager soon after and, of course, we all know the success he had!

Sarah Decent

Brentford are my nemesis. They raise my blood pressure more than our supposed local rivals. I've never seen us win a game at Brentford (in eight visits as of January 2003). I'll keep going until we do. Brentford away holds numerous outstanding memories. Support the like of which I have never heard before or since during the 1-1 draw in April 1994. Paul Gibbs receiving the red card after kicking a Brentford player up in the air in a moment that typified his spell at Argyle. But these take a back seat to another glorious afternoon at Griffin Park, on Saturday 17 December 1994. The 7-0 defeat (the *Grandstand* videprinter would have spelt it out in brackets next to the number) at Brentford said everything about the club at the time – great support; a team at odds with each other and the management; and a management and board without dignity or respect. Never has a game and result so aptly summed up a season. We had already lost 5-1 at home to them in the opening home match. Brentford finished second that season, but they were out of form when we met them at Griffin Park. They had just one win in their previous seven League games. At that point, we did not know the full story behind Shilton and McCauley's soap opera. But it was common knowledge that the relationship had collapsed, a team that had been fantastic the previous season was hopeless this time, and that unless the team turned it around sharply, Shilton was on his way out. After all, in their all-too-public staring contest, the manager was always going to blink before the guy holding the purse strings. A few days before, Peter Shilton had been signing books in a Plymouth bookshop. In the light of an injury crisis, and from lack of anything else to say to a footballer (rarely first choice to provide stimulating conversation), I had asked who would be playing at left-back that Saturday against Brentford. Shilton joked that he didn't know and that I should bring my boots. Looking at the scoreline, you may think that I had. I've seen Argyle get beaten many times. Well beaten. But this was so comprehensive as to remove the supporter from the normal reactions to a thrashing. It was more than simple errors in play or superior opposition. It was utter capitulation, which allowed us supporters to distance ourselves and to smile at the absurdity. Initially, perhaps until the fourth Brentford goal went in, I felt the usual combination of anger, misery and self-loathing. That changed as the match drifted into the surreal. I can vividly remember singing 'Nil-six to the Argyle' with a smile on my face. The feeling returned at the end, as we all waved to the manager as the team sloped off, and sang: 'Bye-bye Shilton, Shilton bye'. We knew he was doomed. He must have too. The story of the match itself is only worth telling to embellish the statistics. As soon as Plymouth were a couple of goals down after 8 minutes, any belief and hope and determination, which was in short supply in the first place, evaporated totally. They couldn't string passes together, played too much hit-and-hope, and no one wanted to take responsibility and hold on to the ball. In contrast, Brentford took appropriate advantage of a team in disarray. The score was only 2-0 at half-time. Most, if not all of us, did not expect Argyle to make a comeback, not with the goal-shy front line of Evans and Ross. But a cricket score was not a foregone conclusion. Annon and Smith had given Brentford the comfortable half-time lead. In the second half, Martin Hodge in the Plymouth goal had a 'mare, showing his age with hesitation, poor handling and no command of his area. The inexperienced Dawe played at right-back, cruelly introduced to League football amidst a collapsible defence, marshalled by the woefully unpopular and uninspiring Peter Swan – a totem of the excesses and egotism of the later McCauley/Shilton era. Taylor, with a couple, Forster, Mundee and Harvey helped themselves to goals. If the game had carried on, they would have

kept on scoring. The game was significant to me from a supporter's perspective. It reflected what is good and bad about supporting Plymouth, or indeed any team. It was a microcosm of the supporter's experience. Football is not just about formations and team selection: 'when are we going to sign a decent goalscorer?' (incidentally, when ARE we going to sign a decent goalscorer?) or 'should Baggins or Bobbins play up front?'. It's what match reports can't convey. It's what watching it on the television can't convey. It's celebrating being a supporter of your team. It's going to a game to say 'Look at us, we support Plymouth, we're proud'. At the end of the match, I was embarrassed by Argyle, humiliated by the overpaid bums and mercenaries in my team. But I was still proud to be a Plymouth supporter. It is games and days like this that make the memorable victories and promotions all the sweeter.

Toby Jones

I always remember the FA Cup game against Everton in 1989. We went 1-0 up through Sean McCarthy midway through the first half, and Everton equalised with a dubious penalty by Kevin Sheedy in the second half. The decision was debatable, as the majority thought Adrian Burrows had been pushed into the ball. I always remember this man holding on to the roof support and standing on the crush barrier to my right singing his head off. I also fell off the crush barrier backwards when we scored, although luckily Dad caught me (I was only young then)!

Benjie Ward

Argyle 4 Manchester United 1. That's some scoreline, isn't it? Try also to imagine that it is a FA Cup third-round tie, coming shortly after an earlier League clash at Home Park, in which Argyle triumphed 3-1. The fact is that it happened. OK – it might have been a few years ago – in 1932 to be precise, but it happened. Season 1931/32 was a great campaign for Argyle, a season in which they were to finally achieve fourth place in the old Second Division, scoring 100 League goals in the process. Manchester United, however, were struggling. Not surprisingly, Argyle were favourites to go through to the next round, particularly as they had already turned United over in the League. Apparently, it was thought that the Argyle supporters felt it was a foregone conclusion, and this is one explanation for a disappointing attendance of 28,000. Plymouth's last home fixture had been against fellow promotion contenders Bury, a League game that had attracted over 36,000 and saw Argyle coast home 5-1. But on Saturday 9 January 1932, the weather was atrocious – driving rain and high winds. That must also have been a factor in the poor attendance. The match went as predicted. One report said: 'Argyle's footwork continually had the United defenders struggling to turn as the ball was manoeuvred past them ... the rain continued to pour and the ground became heavier, but Argyle kept up the momentum ... the United goal, 3 minutes from time, was only a token effort ... the younger, fitter home side made light of the conditions.' At the end of the game, a United director was quoted as saying he envied the home side and wished United were as good. Times change ... Another great match was Arsenal 4 Plymouth Argyle 2. My father,

now in his mid-nineties, started following Argyle at the beginning of the First World War. When we meet up, he still reminisces about the 'Greats' who wore the green shirt, and also recalls some of the memorable matches. He often chuckles about the way, as a young lad, he somehow managed to scale the trees overhanging the Barn Park End and drop into the ground without paying! With the passing years, his recollections have understandably become punctuated with pauses while he struggles to remember a player's name or position. But when he talks of the Argyle visit to Highbury in January 1932 for an FA Cup fourth round clash, there is no hesitation or long-term memory loss. The fact is that he was there, together with another 65,385 who paid out the astronomical sum of £4,539 18s! Both teams were up for it. Arsenal were the current First Division Champions and had knocked in eleven goals against Darwen in the previous round. Argyle, who were mounting a serious bid for promotion to join the Gunners in the First Division, had already disposed of Manchester United 4-1 in the third round, and had thrashed Millwall 8-1 on the previous Saturday. Half-an-hour before the kick-off, the gates were closed. Those fainting on the packed terraces were passed down to the front over the heads of other spectators. Highbury crackled with tension. After only 5 minutes, Argyle were in front! Clever work by winger Tommy Crozier set up Jack Leslie, who rattled the Arsenal crossbar. Jack Vidler, following up, put the ball in the net. To their credit, Argyle continued to take the game to the home side and had two confident penalty appeals ignored. Sammy Black and Vidler both went close in trying to extend Plymouth's lead. But after 33 minutes, Arsenal drew level with a goal that bore more than a hint of offside. Half-time: 1-1. Within 3 minutes of the re-start, two Argyle players, George Reed and Jack Pullen, were both injured and carried off. Arsenal were digging in. Both players returned, Reed's head swathed in heavy bandages. With 20 minutes to go, it was still 1-1. A replay at Home Park? Jack Lambert, the Arsenal forward, had other ideas. Leaving the Argyle defence, plead-ing for offside, behind him, he went on to tuck the ball past Bill Harper. Within 4 minutes, the Gunners had made it 3-1, with Joe Hulme finding the net. Back came Argyle, Jack Leslie was on target. 3-2 – game on! Ten minutes remained and Argyle were still in there, battling. Then – tragedy. Plymouth defender Harry Roberts, from just outside the penalty area, put through his own net, lobbing the Argyle 'keeper who, a month earlier, had been on Arsenal's books. What apparently had endeared the Argyle side to the home fans was their positive, attacking style of play, and those who had made the long journey up from the West Country returned with their heads held high. Arsenal went on to Wembley without conceding another goal. Argyle finished the season in fourth place in the Second Division, which still remains their highest ever League position.

Nigel Springthorpe

Probably the Darlington game in the 2001/02 season. It was a great feeling winning the Championship, as I'm sure success always feels ten times better when you support an average side and they win something, rather than being an Arsenal fan and being pretty sure of winning at least one trophy each season. I might revise that in a few years time when we're topping the Premiership and dominating the Champions' League! Rather a strange feeling though, running around at a foot-ball match in a leather skirt and high heels, à la Susie Reynolds. I think I shall be stick-ing to shorts in future.

Martin Brock

Argyle 3 Port Vale 2 in 1977. A relegation decider – a game of unbelievable tension. Vale scored first after 2 minutes. Brian Johnson equalised, and I think Fred Binney got the other two. There was a pitch inva-sion at the end, with Malcolm Allison hailed as the saviour.

David Whitehouse

I witnessed two League Cup semi-final home legs against Leicester City and Manchester City. Both games were drawn, with Argyle losing the away legs. I was very young at the time, but can still remember Gordon Banks making a bril-liant save at the Devonport End from either Cliff or Alex Jackson. I also saw the 3-1 win against Stoke City in an earlier round. Unfortunately, the legendary Stanley Matthews, who was still playing at the time, didn't make the game. Other Argyle legends in that team were Johnny Newman, Tony Book and Barrie Jones, Malcolm Allison being the manager. Steve Davey scored in the 1-1 draw with Man City. It was a weekday afternoon kick-off, due to a national power strike. Devonport Dockyard had shut down early to prevent a massive sick-note epidemic! So there was a mass exodus of yardies at lunchtime, heading for pubs and the ground. Alan Welsh and Ernie Machin were key members of Tony Waiters' team in the great FA Cup run that season. City had Colin Bell, Francis Lee and Denis Law in their line-up. Both games were fantastic occasions and were significant in that Argyle fans were given a tantalising sniff of the big-time.

Pete Colbourne

It was Manchester City away in '87 or '88, when we had that good season in the First Division. It was my first PASALB trip and, other than Argyle losing (2-0 or 2-1), it was pretty much a perfect day. The day was full of all that is good about following a football team in good company. Mind you, winning at cards on the way up and on the return trip did add some polish! The conversation was sport in general, as well as football and Argyle in particular. The old Irish saying of a stranger being a friend you had not met yet was never so true. Fifteen years later, I'm still happily going to away games. That one trip has made a lasting impression. Then there was Mansfield away in the 2001/02 season. It showed so clearly that the entire character of Plymouth Argyle had changed. Being under the cosh like that was normally the sign of a hammering to come. We held out, but what really showed that times were changing was firstly getting the 'last-minute sickener' against the run of play (we never do that!) and secondly getting another (what is going on?). When Sturrock walked off the pitch, he looked at the fans going wild and shook his head as if to say: 'It was a bit of a fluke, not the crushing win you're making it out to be.' But I think he missed the point (he was still new, after all). We just don't do performances like that, lucky ones that is, and the fact that we did brought belief to the hope that it would be our year.

John Williams

11 September – one of those dates that none of us will ever forget. Wedding anniversaries will be forgotten and family birthdays will be missed, but 11 September is one of those dates that will be forever etched on our memories. For most people, this has been the case since the unforgettable and shocking events in New York City in 2001 but for me, at the risk of being seen as flippant, the date has been memorable since 1973. I came home from school as usual, got changed, had my tea and sat down with my brother to watch the great Don Arnold on Westward Television's *Sports Desk*. Argyle had had a poor start to the season, with just one point gained from the first three games, and manager Tony Waiters was expected to ring the changes for Rochdale's visit to Home Park. However, when Don told us of these changes, we were shocked, as not only was the manager bringing in three untried youngsters, but he was dropping the great Jimmy Hinch to make way for one of them. Watching Argyle at that time had become pretty dismal. On the face of it, we had enough good players in the squad – Ernie Machin, Steve Davey and Alan Welsh for example – to be challenging for promotion back to the Second Division, but the team was not performing consistently and there were too many weak links. One of these was Jimmy Hinch. He was a gangling

6ft 2in centre forward who had been signed from Tranmere by Ellis Stuttard in a swap deal, which had seen centre half Fred Molyneux move in the opposite direction. There were occasional moments of brilliance from big Jim, like his winner in the third round of the cup against Middlesbrough in 1972/73. This earned us a fourth-round trip to Elland Road to meet Leeds, who were, at that time, one of the most feared clubs in Europe, not least for their physical approach to the game epitomised by the likes of Norman Hunter and Billy Bremner. This was the scene of one of Argyle's most memorable FA Cup matches, as the Greens matched Leeds and only went out 2-1 as a result of a fumble by the usually reliable Jim Furnell and another Leeds goal that looked suspiciously offside. It also saw the other, darker side of Hinchy as, with no thought of the terrible retribution he might face from Don Revie's hired thugs, he laid out the Leeds 'keeper David Harvey, but managed to escape without so much as a booking. He had a way of getting away with the most astonishing assaults on opposing players, not least, I fancy, because of the almost constant look of serene innocence on his face, which may have appeared to some to be the result of mental inadequacy. Hinchy has gone on to be a highly successful and wealthy businessman in the USA, by the way, so I suspect there may have been some method in his madness. This mixture of brilliance, brutality and beatitude made Hinchy something of a folk hero at Home Park. I recall one particularly vicious assault on a full-back during the course of one of the series of ill-tempered matches between Argyle and Port Vale in the early Seventies. Big Jim launched himself from about 5 yards away at his target, made full

contact and left the poor chap writhing in agony on the cinder track after he had collided with the iron railings. The referee was quickly on the scene, but the big fella amazingly escaped with a lecture and lolloped away (Jim never ran, he always lolloped) with a smile on his face. Harley Lawer got into the spirit of the thing when he described the incident in the *Sunday Independent* the following day, something along the lines of 'The Vale defender was stretchered off after a comprehensive tackle by Jimmy Hinch' – not a foul you understand, a 'comprehensive tackle'. He was nothing if not entertaining, and now he was to be dropped from the side to be replaced by some young whippersnapper with no League experience. So there we were, on the terraces at Home Park on a misty night in early autumn, bemoaning the lack of experience in the side and wondering how long it would be before the manager saw sense and recalled the great man. The game kicked off and, 45 minutes later, the terraces were buzzing. Argyle were running rings around Rochdale, the three youngsters having already made an impact. Brian Johnson on the right wing and Alan Rogers on the left were giving the Rochdale full-backs a real chasing and providing the ammunition for the strikers, local hero Steve Davey and the other new boy – Paul Mariner. I've seen a few decent debuts by Argyle players in my time – David Kemp and the tragic Peter Middleton spring immediately to mind – but these were experienced players who'd come to the club with reputations. This was something entirely different, a young striker who was so obviously destined for bigger things, but who had come into the side almost unheralded. Everyone within earshot was convinced we were watching a future England international – it really was that obvious, even to my 15-year-old eyes. Mariner finished the match with two goals. Alan Rogers scored one and Brian Johnson, despite not getting on the score-sheet, played a major part in Argyle's 5-0 win. Mariner also hit the woodwork (he was never to score a hat-trick for Argyle, surprisingly) and generally scared the wits out of Rochdale's defenders. Those of us who were lucky enough to be there will never forget it. I've seen bigger wins, I've seen us promoted and relegated quite a few times, I've seen us win the Division Three Championship, I've seen us win at Wembley, I've seen us win an FA Cup quarter-final against all the odds, I've seen us play against Santos with Pele, I've seen us in an FA Cup semi-final and a League Cup semi-final, I've seen games of high drama and I've seen highly controversial games, but I don't think I've ever walked out of Home Park feeling the way I did that night. I'd just seen something very special and I knew it.

Neil Jenkins

I remember seeing some games involving Jack Rowley during his time as player-manager when I lived in the London area. One match was at Fulham, where the hosts included Johnny Haynes and Jimmy Hill. On another occasion at Brentford, the crowd for the Easter 1959 fixture was so great, I had just reached the turnstile when the gate behind us was closed. The turnstile was also closed as the ground was so full. They eventually let us in after the match had started, but it was hopeless. We couldn't see the game and had to come out at half-time. We returned home only to

Paul Mariner – arguably the best striker ever to have played for the Pilgrims.

learn that Argyle had lost 3-0. In those days, I hardly ever saw Argyle win – let alone score. There was an exception. In January 1967, I was at Millwall for a game where Argyle had not won away all season, and Millwall were undefeated at home for a record number of games. With John Mitten making his debut, Argyle out-played the opposition to win 2-1. Even the goal that Millwall scored was quite obvi-ously offside, but the referee seemed to be not brave enough to disallow it. The scenes after the match from the Millwall crowd were nothing short of disgraceful and the Argyle coach was pelted with stones.

Kenneth Griffin

A friend of mine who was getting married decided to hold his stag do in Chester, as Argyle were playing there and it seemed a good place to spend the weekend away. Ten of us descended on the Friday night, went out and got drunk. Obviously, some beers went down before the game and we got into the ground with a few minutes to spare. Somewhere between the game kicking off and Argyle going 1-0 up, we had all agreed to run on the pitch (in good humour, you understand!) if Argyle scored. When it came down to it, the reality was rather different. Dwight Marshall obliged with the goal, a cracker from a great move. The best man started for the fence, followed by the groom-to-be. Everyone else stayed where they were. The next few minutes are a slight blur as I was laughing like I have never laughed before. The best man, Steve, lumbered on to the pitch towards the celebrating players. Dwight saw him coming and opened his arms. As Steve stepped onto the turf, his legs went from underneath him. He slid forward, straight into Dwight Marshall, taking out his family jewels *en route*. The result was a mass of Argyle players on top of my friend Steve and a writhing-in-agony Dwight. Both Steve and Jason, the groom, got led away for the duration of the game, but apparently the police couldn't stop laughing. It was obvious no harm had been intended. Even Kevin Hodges said words to that effect. Subsequently, Steve was interviewed by telephone on *Soccer AM* about the incident and I am reliably informed that it has also been shown in the What Happened Next? Round on *A Question of Sport*. Maybe it doesn't sound as funny described here, but it was without doubt, the funniest thing I have seen in a football ground.

Jeremy Wilcox

Many of the 38,000 that were at the Argyle v. Santos game on 14 March 1973 will remember it as one of the most wonderful matches ever seen at Home Park – not least because Argyle more than equalled their famous opponents and won 3-2. None of the assembled thousands on the terraces, and only one or two of we backroom staff, had any inkling of the drama taking place in the Argyle boardroom caused by a last-minute demand for an extra £2,000 cash over and above the agreed guarantee, or Santos would not play. Even if Robert Daniel and his board had meekly acceded to this blackmail, there was still no gate money cash readily available as some of us had spent all day on the previous Sunday morning manning the turnstiles to sell advance tickets – the resulting monies having already been banked. For some years, my duties had mainly been dealing with the directors' box, the media and the dressing rooms, handing out complimentary programmes, obtaining team lists and entering the same on a board on the green room wall, so I had no knowledge of these events. Armed with programmes for the Santos team, plus one of my own (incidentally, priced at ten pence), I knocked on the door and entered the dressing room just after seven o'clock, having noticed through the open Argyle dressing room door that our players had changed. On entering the room, I was astounded to see the Santos players all fully dressed – two or three bouncing footballs, some lounging on the seats along the walls, all seemingly disinterested. Like many soccer fans, I was especially interested to meet the great Pelé (partly because my wife had demanded I obtain his autograph) and noticed that he was laying in a position of repose on one of the benches – eyes closed, hands behind his head and legs up against the wall. My enquiries for team names only drew broken English replies of 'Non Inglise', 'Non comprendez' etc., so I withdrew and headed for the boardroom, where Mrs Rita Daniel brought out the Santos chairman, who informed me that the goalkeeper, Claudio, spoke English. Still ignorant of the cause of the hold-up, I went back through the green room, past the anxious gentlemen of the press and once more into the dressing room to find the goalkeeper reclining on the far wall seat. By this time it was 7.15 p.m. – kick off was due at 7.30 p.m.! Gradually, I managed to co-operate with the goalkeeper in compiling a list of players, when, suddenly, the door opened and a South American gentleman entered, rattled off a few words in Portuguese and everyone immediately came to life, making for the kit neatly piled on the treatment table. As I thanked the goalkeeper, who incidentally told me 'no autographs until the game finish', Pelé passed us to collect his number 10 shirt from the table. I asked him if he would sign my programme after the game, upon which he shook my hand and said 'for you – now'. I still have the programme. So all was well that ended well, although it was a long time before Argyle were repaid their £2,000 after appeals to FIFA. Incidentally, the many photographs of smiling and friendly faces taken at a post-match get-together at a city centre hotel seemed to be in direct contrast to the pre-match ill-feeling and anxieties.

Lou Weeks

A trip to Chesterfield, and I wasn't very happy with the omens. Chesterfield had reached the sixth round of the FA Cup,

Southampton were stalking Michael Evans and Argyle were playing without a spine, for Heathcote, Barlow and Littlejohn were all injured. It felt like roll-over time as I took my bench-space. Bruce Grobelaar, however, seemed jovial enough, and I wondered just what obscure antics he would demonstrate this time. I wasn't happy with the referee either. At first, it was his enviable suntan. This was unacceptable in Chesterfield. Bruce had been known to jet in from Zimbabwe and Carlo from Canadian matches, but this official had flown in on the night before the game from a vacation abroad. He was to referee in misty, drizzly Chesterfield; no doubt the highlight of his week. The official was not going to allow Argyle to employ a captain. Once he was sure that Heathcote was injured and unavailable, he targeted stand-in skipper Ronnie Maugé. Around the half-hour mark, the midfielder's control deserted him, the ball broke loose and as he challenged Beaumont, Mauge's feet slipped (honestly!) and caused a two-footed tackle. The opponent feigned death, the referee saw his opportunity and, with a jubilant sneer, dismissed Maugé. Logan was next on the hit-list. The captain's armband highlighted Logan's towering defensive performance, frustrating the match official, who was vainly searching for a reason to dispose of another Pilgrim skipper. Salvation was provided by Darren Carr, a crooked Spire-ite if ever I saw one, and doubtless the referee's hit-man. He hammered Bruce, careered into Curran and began the mêlée in which young Chesterfield striker Kevin Davies was to provoke Logan into evasive and bar-room action. A referee's assistant officiated this bout, reported the wild fists and gutter rolls to the referee and thus Argyle's third skipper bit the dust! I never did find out who captained the team for the final seconds, but I reckon it was Illman, who was sneakily substituted to confuse the referee and prevent another mouth-watering sending-off! I was not impressed with one over-ripe referee's assistant either, who demonstrated quite an ability in semaphore signalling, then an irritating need to grin at the agitated Argyle fans as they admonished his decisions. I was really happy that Ronnie Maugé had taken a seat in the stand though, for had he still been playing, the brawl might have been even more embittered. It was difficult to tell, however, whether he was being restrained from leaping out of the upper tier to 'join the lads'! I was really ecstatic about the team's commitment and performance, however, outplaying a sluggish and unimaginative Chesterfield outfit. The victory was deserved and emotional, but I shall never forget the scenes when Tony James was dismissed – and he wasn't even wearing a captain's armband. He was given a marvellous exit by the fans and returned the compliment, bowing in worship to the supporters. Admittedly, he had just won the main bout, stopping Darren Carr with a flurry of punches, pinning his opponent against the inside of the goal net! At the final whistle, the celebrations resembled Wembley and somehow, I believe that the players and fans became closer in this adversity. Despite the omens, pride won the day and the referee was left to scour the ground for a certain tell-tale armband.

Pete Ray

The Battle of Saltergate.

It is easy to write about the famous occasions in recent times, like. the Wembley play-off final or the FA Cup semi-final at Villa Park, but my abiding memory of Argyle goes back to season 1973/74. With victories over Torquay (2-0), Portsmouth (4-0), Burnley (2-1), QPR (3-0) and Birmingham City (2-1), Argyle had made it to the semi-final of the Football League Cup against the might of Manchester City. Here was a team that consisted of the likes of Colin Bell, Francis Lee, Mike Summerbee, Denis Law and Rodney Marsh, plus many, many more stars. Argyle, on the other hand, also had its great stars – well, I thought so anyway – Jim Furnell, Johnny Hore, Bobby Saxton, Steve Davey, Ernie Machin and, of course, Paul Mariner. Could we beat the mighty Manchester City? Of course we could, we're the famous Plymuff Argyle and we're going to Wemb-a-lee! The game was played on 23 January with a kick-off time of 2 p.m. on a wet Wednesday afternoon, due to the three-day week and power cuts that the country was going through at the time. We were told at school that we could go to the match, if our parents provided us with a note. Out of my class of about thirty, I think only two or three didn't go to the game. The register the next day ended up about a foot thick with all the notes. I managed to get to Home Park reasonably early, trying to get any autographs that I could (I wish I could find that autograph book, it would be worth a fortune nowadays). I tried to get as near to the front as I could – I'm not the tallest of people – with my programme in hand, ready for the game. Within the programme, there was a semi-final song written by a local musician. The first verse was:

Plymouth,
Plymouth
Argyle,
Argyle
We will win
In good and grand style,
We'll go on to victory
Plymouth
Plymouth Argyle.

It didn't quite make it on to *Top of the Pops*! Over 30,000 were at Home Park for the match, and I'm afraid this is the time when my memory starts to let me down. I think Argyle scored first through Steve Davey, but I'm putting my lack of memory down to the fact that I couldn't see most of the game, because I couldn't get to the front and had to stand behind this lanky so-and-so. Anyway, the game eventually ended up as a 1-1 draw and we WERE going to Wemb-a-lee. Oh, the joys of being young and confident about your football team (now I'm older and wiser, I still think we'll get to Wemb-a-lee, the European Cup Final, Premier League Championship etc. etc.) A week later, we were beaten 2-0 at Maine Road.

Terry Guswell

Plymouth Argyle's David Kemp headed the ball towards goal. Chester goalkeeper Grenville Millington stretched to make the save. He knocked the ball away and collided with an upright. The goalpost snapped near its base, the crossbar swung freely and the net caved in. Kemp thought he had scored. Millington was too dazed to know. That broken goalpost caused the first leg of the Chester-Plymouth League Cup first-round tie to be abandoned after

78 minutes. It became one of the few two-legged League Cup ties to need a replay after the first leg. The score at that time was 2-2, Kemp having started the scoring, Steve Ludlam managing two for Chester and John Sims squaring the scores, just a few minutes before the goal collapsed. The teams met at Chester the following week. The replay had one goal each in the first half, and they each had a goal to defend through the whole game – rather than for just 78 minutes. Another 1,700 spectators turned out (or was it the same 1,700 as the previous week?) but Chester had to fork out for a new goal and Plymouth bore the costs of another round trip of 500 miles.

Dave Gadd

Plymouth Argyle were at Barrow and there were 13 minutes to play. Then came a goal to settle the game, scored by the most unlikely person on the pitch – referee Ivan Robinson. Barrow won a corner and the ball was cleared. George McLean shot hard from outside the penalty area and the ball was going well wide. Referee Robinson, perhaps 15 yards from goal, was in the path of the ball. He jumped up to avoid it, but the ball hit him on the inside of his left foot and flew off at an angle. Plymouth goalkeeper Pat Dunne was completely deceived by the deflection. Having moved to cover McLean's shot, Dunne was stranded as the ball shot past him and into the net. Barrow 1 (the referee) Plymouth Argyle 0. The rules are quite clear: the ball is in play if it rebounds off either the referee or linesman when they are on the field of play. Ivan Robinson knew that. He pointed meekly to the centre circle to confirm his goal. The Plymouth players looked stunned and shocked. The incident spurred Argyle into a frenzied late rally, but Barrow hung on to win, and the referee had to avoid congratulatory pats on the back from Barrow supporters as he ran off the field.

Andrew Ward

I remember my dad and granddad telling me about it – they don't make games like that any more. It was in the bitter winter of 1960 that Argyle visited the monster stadium that was The Valley, for a Boxing Day Second Division clash. Barely 11,196 graced the terraces that could hold 60,000 people. Argyle were still reeling from their last League game at Stoke on 17 December, where they had gone down to a record 9-0 defeat! Leading the Argyle line that day were the great Wilf Carter and George Kirby. The latter stole the thunder, scoring twice as we went down 6-4, Anderson and Johnny Williams poaching the other two. For the rematch at Home Park on the very next day, Kirby was injured, and a young man, name of Johnny Brown, was drafted in for his debut. Brown had a blinder, but Carter was the one that went down in the Argyle record books when he scored four plus a penalty (the fifth) – a feat unequalled in a League game before or since. Jackson got the other goal. As a point of interest, the gate that day for a mid-table team after 3 straight defeats and 18 goals conceded was a whopping tally of 23,335. It's amazing what no decent television on a Boxing Day does for football crowds.

Mark Smith

Argyle 3 Colchester 1 – the second leg of the 1996 play-off semi-final. Neil Warnock had never had to reverse an aggregate scoreline, but at one down after the first meeting, he had to. So that sun-baked Wednesday came, and to say I was worried would be an understatement. For me, nothing had ever hinged on one game for Argyle as it had now. Would we be creative enough to open up a stubborn Colchester defending a 1-0 lead? Would we give away an early goal? I had been to one play-off semi-final before, against Burnley two years earlier, and how I'd love to go over that one again, but hey, I think we'll go on. We took up our positions in an atmospheric Devonport End. It's on nights like these when this particular end really shines out – flags, colour, full volume from all parts of the ground. We were staring fate full on in the face. The whistle blew. Argyle started off well. Barlow had been chosen to play on the right wing. Suddenly, Evans was put through. We watched, expecting him to waste it. But then he lifted it over the keeper. GOAL! We had levelled the aggregate score. Play continued. Argyle were on full attack, Barlow launching a personal vendetta against a nervous Colchester defence, playing at his superb best. Still we waited for another breakthrough. Then came a free-kick just outside the penalty box on the right-hand side. What had Argyle practised in training? Despite Trigger's goal, I was still somewhat pessimistic. Then came a vicious, curling shot. IT'S IN! WE'RE AHEAD ON THE NIGHT! Could this be the night? My feelings were changing, but still I felt reluctant to join in the chants of 'We're going to Wembley, you're not'. Argyle continued to press, Colchester showing more purpose,

but still somewhat restrained. Barlow continued to wreak havoc on that right wing. I'm sure the Colchester defence were prepared to let him right through on goal on a couple of occasions. Argyle pressed more and more, looking for that decisive third goal. Littlejohn was felled on the edge of the box, clean through on goal. Surely a Colchester player would walk? But no, the yellow card was produced. Warnock was not accepting this, venting his rage on an unsuspecting linesman (they were called linesmen then!). The referee was brought over, and what must have been the entire Plymouth support let him know exactly what they thought of him. I'll never forget that volume of noise. So Warnock was ordered off the touchline, but what's this? Is he jumping in with the crowd? This was my enduring memory of Neil, and it's what he can best be remembered for, his passion for the cause and his empathy with the fans. Not 5 minutes had passed from this, when Kinsella unleashed his second fierce long-range shot of the tie, catching out a slowing Argyle defence and an unsuspecting Steve Cherry. Colchester had their away goal. Thoughts of Burnley returned for the first time since kick-off, and confusion reigned in the Devonport End over whether away goals were taken into account before or after extra time. But Argyle were having none of it, pushing Colchester deep into their half, Barlow the ring-leader as ever. Cross after cross poured in. The minutes passed, then Paul 'Charlie' Williams appeared from out of the blue and majestically powered the ball into the back of the net. A brief second passed, then rather like the Coca-Cola advert, the Devonport End rose as one, acknowledging the fact that Argyle were indeed on their way to Wembley. Scarves and flags were waved around manically. The chorus grew. Then the whistle went and the green of the pitch was instantaneously swamped by hordes of fans, singing and shouting. Such relief. The ghost of Burnley had been laid to rest and somehow, after this night, I never really doubted Argyle's ability to win at Wembley.

Anonymous

Argyle v. Bristol City April, 1986. I have read Garry Nelson's thoughts about this game. For the record, he freely admits he does not remember much about the goal he scored, but it was a great one. I was standing in front of the Mayflower Stand, totally trapped by the press of bodies roaring Argyle on to promotion. The most vivid memory for me was the gradual movement of the Lyndhurst fans, creeping over the fence as the 90 minutes was coming close. A huge buzz went around the ground as word was passed of Wigan's demise. The final 5 or 10 minutes of the game were played near the tunnel as the press of fans crowded the far touchline. The ref blew about 3 or 4 minutes before the 90 minutes were up, and every player made a mad dash for the tunnel. Great game, great memories and promotion to boot.

James Dennis

WBA 2 Plymouth Argyle 5, April 1993. It was with disbelief that I forced myself to go to watch a pointless match for Argyle against promotion-chasing West Bromwich Albion. Two days earlier, we had suffered

the ultimate humiliation, losing 3-0 at home to E*eter. The sight of Alan Ball running up and down the touchline and season ticket books being thrown onto the pitch was almost too much. The 1992/93 season itself had been a joke. Newly relegated, we expected so much. Peter Shilton's first full season in charge, and with so much spent on new players, surely we should have done better than mid-table. Yet sadly for me, I bleed green blood, and I can NEVER see me giving in on the love of my life. West Brom were going up, if not automatically, then certainly through the play-offs. Ossie Ardiles had seen his side win 7 home games in a row, so surely we didn't stand a chance. 16,000 fans cheered as the expected happened, Taylor put the Baggies 1-0 up. But then, something amazing happened – Castle equalised. This was surely a minor hiccup! But no, Castle scored a lovely second and at half-time, we were 2-1 up. We expected a bag of goals in the second half, but from West Brom! Incredibly, Castle drilled in his hat-trick and I was in dream land! Why? It was a nothing game, but my love for Argyle was taking over. Dalton scored a fourth, and then, after taking the mick out of West Brom's goalkeeper Lange, Barlow added the fifth. Although Donovan pulled one back, this was the most memorable game I had ever seen. It is games like this that make it all worthwhile. As for West Brom, they went to Wembley and beat Port Vale in the play-off final and Peter Swan was sent off!

Bob Banister

Stockport 2 Plymouth 4, 1994. Having watched Argyle since 1983 and seen

Promotion is sealed in fine style as Bristol City are crushed 4-0 at Home Park in 1986.

some breathtaking games, such as the home FA Cup tie against Everton (1-0 up, remember?), and being 2-0 down at half-time to Manchester City in the old Second Division and coming back to win the game 3-2, the game that will always stick in my mind was this one. Being a student in Manchester, it was just down the road. It was pouring with rain, but there was a good turnout. Within 30 seconds of the kick-off, Stockport had scored and everyone supporting Argyle just wanted to go home. These were the days when Kevin Francis was playing for Stockport and we had Alan Nicholls in goal. At half-time we had taken the lead 2-1, but it was the second half that proved almost too much for the old heart. When the score got to 3-2, Alan Nicholls was booked for time-wasting. In true Alan style, he threw a HUGE strop and just

threw the ball away in front of the referee, who had no hesitation in booking him again and dismissing him from the field. James Dungey was brought on as a substitute and Stockport were trying to take full advantage of his size by just crossing the ball into the box towards Francis. We just knew that they had to score eventually. It was just a matter of time. For about 15 minutes, it was a nightmare to watch – they were bound to draw level – when, all of a sudden, the ball reached the half-way line and Richard Landon ran the whole way, rounded the 'keeper and neatly tucked it away for 4-2. I don't think I've ever seen Argyle fans go so mad. Soaking wet, but thrilled to bits, that's how I remember leaving Edgely Park that day.

Richard Hoskin

47

Pompey 0 Argyle 3, 12 September 1989. Living in Portsmouth for the past twelve years and with all my workmates knowing how much I support Argyle, it is of the utmost importance to me that the Greens put up a good account of themselves whenever they come to town. On this occasion, I was invited by a friend, who also happened to be a Portsmouth sponsor, to be his guest at the game. Along with the invitation came the normal Pompey bravado, and I heard non-stop for days beforehand how we didn't have a chance. Portsmouth, after all, were a good home side. We took our seats in the directors' box amongst the Pompey faithful, me with my green scarf tucked in my coat pocket, as I was told that it wasn't really the done thing to wear it! The highlight of the first half was Tommy Tynan scoring. This would normally signal a Pompey backlash and revival, but for some reason that day, it never happened. Over the half-time tea and biscuits, my companion assured me that the game wasn't over yet. From my experiences of watching Argyle, I knew that he was right. I thought it best to retain a dignified silence to save any potential embarrassment later. The second half kicked off and I awaited the immediate Pompey reply, which surprisingly never came. In fact, it was Argyle who scored twice more in the second half, through Tynan and Andy Thomas. At this point, my companion left me, hurdling the barrier into the main stand. He returned several minutes later looking a little more satisfied. Apparently, loudly shouting abuse at your own players doesn't go down too well in the directors' box either! After the game, we were escorted into the bar for a (in my case, celebratory) drink. You could have heard a pin drop. Not even the raffling of

a football signed by the Pompey team could muster any enthusiasm, Liverpool scoring ten against Crystal Palace was greeted with a barely audible sigh. I decided to leave them to it. Just in case the autumn weather had severely worsened, I withdrew my Argyle scarf from my coat pocket and made a show of putting it on. I thanked them wholeheartedly for a great day out, bade them farewell and made the 10-minute journey home on foot. The next day it gave me great pleasure to go to work. My green scarf hung majestically over my desk and, to this day, the team sheet still hangs impressively on my pinboard!

Debbie Lloyd

Without checking the records, I cannot tell which season it was, but a match I will never forget was an away game at Peterborough which, I believe, we only needed to draw, but wound up losing 1-0. That day, as so often happens I think, half of Plymouth was in Peterborough and I well remember meeting people that I had not spoken to in years. Old school pals, old workmates, neighbours – the lot. But what a miserable trip home …

Ken Jones

Argyle 4 Swindon 3, Boxing Day 1974. My father had returned to Scotland for the funeral of his eldest brother, so my uncle Fred took me to this match. The whole occasion sticks in my mind because it was the first time I had seen Dad cry, the first (and only) time Dad wasn't home for Christmas and the first time that I had been taken to a match by someone else. And what a match – Argyle in the middle of their unbeaten run against a strong Swindon side, who had beaten Argyle 2-0 earlier in the season. An 18,000-strong crowd buzzed with anticipation, but Argyle got off to a dreadful start and were 2-0 down until just before half-time (both Swindon goals were crackers, to be fair). Then, a free-kick was awarded outside the area at the Devonport End, and Colin Randell chipped a lovely ball, which floated over the 'keeper's head and dropped inside the goal. I always remember the way that it didn't hit the net, but landed, without a bounce, about two feet over the line. Suddenly, we were back, and just after the break John Delve backheaded us level – we were surely on our way. But instead, Swindon took the lead again through an almost carbon copy of their second goal. My spirits sank – my dad away from home and Argyle heading for defeat – how bad could Christmas get for a 9-year-old? But the Immortal took pity and Argyle finished with a barnstorming performance as Billy Rafferty, from a Mariner cross (how often that happened, and how often it was reciprocated in the two seasons they played together), and Mariner, from the penalty spot, gave us the crucial win! When Argyle beat Crystal Palace 2-1 in the second round of the FA Cup, I had to play football for my Boy's Brigade team, so my Dad took my two best mates instead. They talked about it for weeks afterwards. 1-0 down, 2-1 up and then THAT penalty save in the last minute by Jim Furnell from Terry Venables – I remember Brian Moore showing it on *On The Ball* the following week (Argyle were so rarely on the box that even the merest mention used to send me into raptures, so

actual footage – well, you can imagine …). For the 1-1 draw between Argyle and Colchester in November 1980, the *Match of the Day* cameras were at Home Park – it was a dull game and a rainy day, but halfway through the first half came a bizarre accident, as one of the little diddy men that we used to use as ballboys was hit by a ricochet ball and knocked flat out. I am ashamed to say that it happened right in front of me and my friends – we thought it was hilarious and began a mock counting-out (which was captured on the cameras!). Well, it was comical and the little lad was fine afterwards, and things got even better when Kemp got a late equaliser. Jimmy Hill used the whole incident (the knock-out and Kemp's equaliser) to close out the show. I can still remember his closing words '… and then your team scores and the sun comes out again' over the picture of the little lad's smiling facing after the goal. Argyle 0 Huddersfield 0 in March 1981 remains famous in my mind for one marvellous moment from a terrace wag. Halfway through the dreadful second half of a dire game, a fan next to me called over one of the policeman who was pacing around the perimeter and, having got his attention, with the utmost earnestness pointed to an Argyle midfielder and said 'Officer, arrest that man, he's impersonating a footballer'. Argyle 1 Bristol Rovers 0 in March 1974 was my first game from the stands. Dad – a Glaswegian – was a huge Davie Provan fan. We were sitting in front of Len Jackman – remember him and his organ at the Far Post Club? Len kept slagging off Provan throughout the match, and my dad (who had a Glaswegian's temper) was getting more and more restless and irate, muttering darkly and using the word 'bampot' a lot about Mr Jackman. Then, with just a few minutes left, the ball broke free in the Barn Park penalty area and who should blast it home, but Big Dave. Cue my Dad, leaping from his seat and, in a rare and almost graceful pirouette, leaping round and screaming at Len with a gloating sense of victory 'Who scored?! Who scored?! Tell me who scored?!' Answer came there none. Finally, a possibly controversial choice, but surely one of the great soap operas of all time: Argyle 0 Oldham 2, November 1997 – Warnock's return to Home Park. Now I confess to being a Warnock fan – only Smith and Luggy have also delivered the goods in their first full season. Warnock was also a marvellous motivator. Also, I confess to not being a fan of Dan, so I made a special trip down to Plymouth for this game and I further confess my emotions were mixed – I wanted Argyle to win, but I wanted Dan to know how stupid he had been in letting Neil go. The whole day was extraordinary. Warnock came out to a good reception, but three-quarters of the ground couldn't see him because – it seemed to me that Dan had deliberately plotted this – the entrance to the pitch and to the benches were covered by 'match day sponsors and attendants'. Then Oldham played poorly, falling over at every touch, and Warnock was off the bench, screaming at the referee over every potential foul. It was almost as if he was deliberately trying to contrast his passionate commitment to his team with Mick Jones' more reserved manner (and what a subtext there was there between Warnock and his previously loyal lieu-tenant). Then Argyle scored and how ironic that it was Ronnie Maugé – hero of our finest hour with his headed goal at Wembley – who should score it with a

header, and how doubly ironic that it should be into his own net! From then on in, the game was scrappy and fractious, and the referee took centre stage by allow-ing the Oldham players to take their time in recovering from barely substantial tack-les. The mood turned nasty. The referee and Andy Ritchie tried to joke about their shared follically-challenged conditions as the Devonport End screamed abusively at the man in black 'you bald b*****d', but it did no good. Then, Oldham scored a second and Warnock was practically on the pitch, punching the air with joy. You could see what this win meant to him, and again, it seemed he was trying to say to Mick Jones, 'you can't motivate players for the big game because you can't share their passion with the crowd'. Unfair, of course, but the sad thing was that he turned a sec-tion of the crowd against him and cries of 'Warnock is a w*****' began to be heard. I felt downcast. Finally, the game was over and Warnock was being ushered from the pitch, but he broke free of the steward and rushed back on to the pitch to applaud the Devonport End who had been chanting against him – sadly, the hand signals they returned were not those of applause. I stood up from the stand and applauded him, really because I thought then and still think now, that he was the best chance we had at the time of ever breaking out of lower League mediocrity. On the way back to London that night, I found myself sitting opposite the ref., Barry Knight. When I asked him if he was the ref., he looked at me as if he thought 'Christ, I hope this isn't going to be a fight!', but I merely wanted to buy him a beer and chat about the game from his perspective. We had three or four beers together, and I found him to be a very knowledgeable and level-headed ref. His view on the game was simple: Argyle lacked discipline, tactics and passion, and there was no point blaming the ref. when the first goal was an own goal! As for Warnock, he said that he was regarded throughout the game as an excellent man manager, a shrewd tactician and a good husbander of resources (I paraphrase, obviously) – he also said he was not the easiest manager to referee! It was a pleasant end to a bitter day.

Andy Milligan

Queens Park Rangers 0 Argyle 3, 20 November 1973. This has got to be one of the best performances ever by an Argyle team, and possibly the very best. QPR were right at the top of the (real) First Division and were basking in the glory of being London's top club. They even had a flag flying at the ground to tell us. Their team was studded with superstars – Parkes, Clement, Hazell, Venables, Mancini, McLintock, Thomas, Francis, Busby, Bowles and Givens. Our boys were an early version of 'Waiters' Wonders', a team yet to achieve anything – Jim Furnell, Colin Randell, Colin Sullivan, John Hore, Bobby Saxton, Neil Hague, Alan Welsh, Steve Davey, Paul Mariner, Ernie Machin and Alan Rogers. It was my first term at university and I went down to the big city with another Argyle fan (Dick Dendle), an Arsenal fanatic and an archaeologist (who had obviously heard about Argyle's tendency to buy has-beens). Both sides played good, on-the-ground football and Argyle had the edge right throughout a goalless first half. Alan Welsh twice went near, and Steve Davey brought the best out of Phil Parkes with a great header. Eight minutes after half-time, Argyle got their just reward when Welsh beat the ageing Frank McLintock with ease and squeezed a shot between Parkes and the near post. Eleven minutes later, this became 2-0, when Paul Mariner won a goalmouth scramble and passed to Steve Davey, who did the honours. This led to QPR substituting Busby with a blond-haired youngster called John Delve. However, it had little effect, as a rampant Argyle got a third through Alan Welsh. The next day's papers printed a picture of Delve watching in despair as the ball entered the net. Argyle obviously impressed him, as he joined us at the end of the season. Some brave Argyle fans started chanting 'Easy, easy' and, much to our surprise, some QPR fans joined in (on their way to the exits). The victory was just one part of a League Cup run which took the Greens all the way to the semis, when they were just edged out by Man City. The following year, 'Waiters' Wonders' won promotion to the old Second Division, where they badly underperformed, sold Mariner and sacked Waiters (a big mistake). For me, the key player in this team was Ernie Machin – a tireless midfielder who could hold on to the ball. Paul Mariner made the headlines, but Ernie set up the chances.

Keith Whitfield

4 Favourite players

For me, Sammy Black was the greatest left-footed player, not only at Plymouth Argyle, but in the whole country. I used to watch him as a child. In those days, I would watch every Saturday match at Home Park, which would be the first team, and, every other week, reserves games. The admission for a first team game was 6d. When I got my first job in London, I was able to see every Argyle match in the capital. One game that stands out was a match at Spurs on Christmas morning, 1935. Sammy Black was absolutely magnificent and scored a marvellous goal. I can also recall Jack Leslie, Argyle's first black player and a cultured player at that. He played his part in building Black's reputation, feeding him with many chances. Another favourite was Jack Cock, who played up front with Black. But I have to look back to when Argyle won promotion in 1930. That was a damn good side. They always had a reputation for playing good football. In those days, my friend and I hardly watched any other team. We picked places between London and where I was going to go at the weekend to watch Plymouth Argyle. I would start the season by looking at the fixtures to see what we could slot in and which arrangements could be altered. Another particular game I remember was at Portsmouth. They came on to the field as if we were nothing. There were still two or three matches to play and we were sure Argyle were going up, but somehow we botched it. We had some lovely times in the 1930s, and soon after the war, we were sure we would be a great force. More recently, of course, there was the game at Wembley. Darlington were a good side, but Argyle had enough to see them off.

Rt Hon. Michael Foot

This has to be the one and only Paul Mariner. I'm not one who says that I saw this guy's genius immediately. At first, I saw him as a useful bag-carrier for Billy-Billy-Billy-Billy-Billy Rafferty. But in the promotion season, he blossomed into a class act, and his ability to control a ball while under pressure and leave the defender for dead was awesome. The strange thing is that I can't remember a chant for Paul, unlike his brother in arms.

Keith Whitfield

This dates back to the time when Ken Brown was the manager and Argyle were playing at Watford, sometime around Christmas. Argyle were overwhelmed, but had two breaks and won 2-1. I cannot remember the year, but I am sure that James played in goal for Watford. The PASALB group had arranged to meet the players at a pub after the game and I decided to go. I had supported Argyle since 1957 and had hardly talked to any players in all those years, except for Peter McParland and Mike Trebilcock when I was autograph hunting. I got talking firstly to Owen Pickard, a squad player who found it hard to break through into the team. He was a very personable young man, naturally a bit piqued at not having a run in the team, which was then in the old Second Division. Then came my big moment – a chat with my hero, Kevin Hodges, a great player and servant of the club. I told him about the best game I had ever seen, when Argyle were away and they skinned Pompey 3-1. I thought he would be pleased with his own form in that match, but he said 'I was on the bench that evening'. To his credit, he said it in an unassuming way – I had met and spoken to my hero, but my memory had faded!

John Dymot

My favourite player, mainly because he became a friend of mine, was Neil Dougall, a wing-half in the 1952 promotion team. This team, I consider, was Argyle's best ever – Shortt, Ratcliffe, Jones, Dougall, Chisholm, Porteous, Astall, Dews, Tadman, Rattray and Govan. Neil had come from Birmingham a couple of seasons earlier.

Norman Adams

I like players that have me on the edge of my seat when they have the ball, players whose one moment of skill or excitement can make the entrance fee worth it. If you

can combine this with someone who is committed, loyal and honest, it's a rare treat. Dwight Marshall is my favourite Argyle player. Dwight's first League game for Plymouth sums up why he was special. I'd seen him score the winner in a pre-season friendly at St Blazey, but these games are rarely a reliable indicator. The first home game of the 1991/92 season was against Barnsley. Dwight was quick and lively, ran intelligently off the ball, and had a good first touch. I had not seen this in an Argyle striker for a long time. We had been subjected to a succession of target men through the 1980s, ranging from good to average to (most commonly) clueless. Finally, we seemed to have a quick striker who could produce the unexpected. Best of all, he scored that day in a 2-1 victory – with an overhead kick! It wasn't the cleanest of strikes, but few Argyle players I had ever watched would even have tried and certainly none would have succeeded. Instant hero. Dwight shone amidst the long-ball tactics of the Kemp era, and then had the advantage of playing in the Shilton team that served up the most exciting football in recent history. He fitted in perfectly. I remember the 'appears from nowhere' near-post header at Dean Court, the hat-trick in the drubbing of Bradford at Valley Parade, the solo goal versus Barnsley in the FA Cup, and the moment of hope in the second play-off game against Burnley. Dwight wasn't the most lethal of finishers: he missed a lot of chances, but he scored plenty as well. He could create them from little or nothing. Plus, he played with a commitment and sense of innocence and fun that enabled him to connect with us on the terraces. Witness the regular grins to the supporters when lining up for a corner. Even after he

Dwight Marshall – one of the most popular and gifted Argyle players of the 1990s.

left the club for the first time, Dwight showed that the affection was mutual. He was in the crowd during a match at Cambridge, had his name chanted once we knew he was present, and willingly signed autographs and chatted after the match. The best testimony to his popularity came at Luton in February 1997 when he was playing for the opposition. Dwight was past his best and he didn't have a great game, but when he was substituted, the packed away end rose from its seats as one to give him standing ovation. The Luton fans were taken aback. It was at a time when the club was in turmoil, and we responded to someone who represented what can be great about football and a football club.

Toby Jones

Tommy Tynan, because you can't fail to be fond of someone who scored so many goals. Ronnie Maugé, for THAT goal against Darlington. Kevin Nugent, as although he wasn't the best, he always seemed to give it his all, and he was a genuinely nice guy off the field if you ever met him.

Martin Brock

It's Dwight Marshall for me. He had electric pace, great awareness and excellent reflexes. I remember when he first arrived at the club and when I first saw him in a green-and-white shirt. It was against Aston Villa in a Tommy Tynan benefit match and, as he was to do so often that season, he lit up an otherwise dull match. His overhead kicks were a touch of the exotic, some-

thing I'd never seen at Argyle before. He was often described as an enigmatic player, and I can see why. He was also accused of wasting his fair share of chances, but then again the majority of these wasted chances were chances that he'd create, and that no one else in our team would have been in the position to take. He wasn't always a favourite with all the managers during his time, and I remember watching him on *Match of the Day* playing for Middlesborough in the First Division on loan when he couldn't even get in our team! His overhead scissor-kick goal on his debut at Home Park in a 2-1 win against Barnsley, his 'Pelé' goal in a 2-0 win at Home Park against Port Vale, and his goal against Barnsley in the FA Cup sum up everything that was good about Dwight.

Colin Buckley

I guess my favourite past player is Steve Castle. For a midfielder, he was, at our level, sheer class. To provide the amount of goals he did and to be an inspirational captain at the same time is something that not many people can supply. He was a kind of poor man's David Platt. Of the current team, I'd say that Graham Coughlan stands out for me. When you hear about how he signed for us – got off a train, signed a contract and got back on a train – and watch his performances, he shows the same no-nonsense approach. It's not often you say this but, as a free transfer, he shows so much pride and passion in wearing the green shirt, he has to be one of the best signings ever.

Chris Prew

John Uzzell, for many years' honest endeavour and for making the very best of his talent. Wholehearted does not do him justice. I remember him specifically, for a big-style upending of John Robertson at the very start of the home FA Cup tie against Derby in 1985. Current favourite: David Friio.

Roger Willis

My favourite player is a difficult choice. John S. Williams had the hardest shot I have ever seen and was a tough tackler. Paul Mariner was probably the classiest player I have seen in Argyle colours. Tommy Tynan was the most reliable goalscorer. Johnny Hore was the hardest working player, and later got the team to the semi-final, but my favourite is probably Kevin Hodges for sheer durability, graft and undoubted skill. I was sorry that his term as manager was not more productive.

Kevin Howarth

Johnny Hore, because every time he took the pitch, he oozed passion for Argyle. I remember him being the only player on the field with a huge great pair of rugby boots on, so that he could keep his feet in the then mudmire that was Home Park! Paul Mariner and Billy Rafferty seemed to be telepathic, each always knew what the other was going to do. Of the current side, it has to be Paul Wotton. He is Captain Marvel: solid as a rock at the back, not afraid to have a pop at goal and he really has got a wicked right foot!

Andy Soper

It has to be my main man Dwight Marshall. He looked cool, had a good touch and was fast, but it was his actions off the pitch that really clinch it, including the time I saw him strolling through town looking pensive, or when he responded to our post-reserve match chanting with a sly wink, or, best of all, having a drink with him down Union Street one drunken Saturday night with my mate Mike. A class act all round.

James Evans

Well, for favourite players of the past, it has to be Steve McCall. He looked assured and comfortable with the ball, and he was a great passer of the ball, always creating space and picking out the front man. Garry Nelson was a great attacking winger and scored some good goals for us in his time here, especially the goal against Bristol City during Dave Smith's promotion year. 'King' Tommy Tynan quite simply knew where the goal was. He was a poacher of the highest quality – a great striker..

Andy Laidlaw

My favourite players are those with real skill, who can change a game with a bit of magic, and for me Paul Dalton was the most exciting Argyle player I've ever seen. He scored some beautiful goals, and there was a real sense that things were about to happen whenever he got the ball. Argyle were the highest-scoring side in England in 1993/94 and he, more than any other player, embodied the spirit in which that team played. Of the current side, Martin Phillips is probably the player who likes to run at the opposition the most, and, as with Dalton, he can provide moments of skill that make going to football worthwhile.

Luke Hildyard

I suppose that I have two players who fit this bill, and for more or less the same reason, but at totally different times. John Craven, when he joined Argyle, was a really classy player and completely altered the team with his marvellous passes. Graham Coughlan, who has been outstanding ever since he arrived at Home Park, and made some fantastic defensive performances, not to mention scored some great sneaky goals at the far post.

Ken Jones

In these days of squad numbers, it may not be quite so important, but when I was a

John Hore. There was Cornish granite in his boots, and he both played and managed at Home Park.

lad, whoever wore the number nine was king: the centre forward. The best player in school was always the centre forward, and although the number 7 'Beckham' shirt may be challenging its supremacy these days, I still reckon the number 9 has a certain magic about it. So who have been the men to grace the famous shirt at Home Park over the years? Before the war there was Jack Cock, still our record goalscorer, and Ray Bowden, who went on to play for Arsenal and England, although I'm not entirely sure whether shirt numbers were worn while these two played for Argyle. In the Forties and Fifties, there were Maurice Tadman and Wilf Carter (who sometimes played at number 8), who both scored a few goals in their time and whose names can still occasionally be heard at Home Park (well, on the Mayflower side of the ground anyway). In my lifetime, there have been many, including a couple of latter day legends – Paul Mariner (still the finest player I've ever seen in the green) and the great Tommy Tynan – plus a few more worthy of mention like local lad Fred Binney. However, despite Mariner's status as the greatest (in my opinion), I am going to name another number 9 as my Argyle hero. As I said, the number 9 shirt had a special significance to it when I was a lad, so it was only natural that the first time I was taken to Home Park, I was going to look out for the centre forward. I could have been unlucky – Frank Lord may have been in the side that day – but as it turned out I was fortunate, as the chosen man on my big day was none other than local hero Mike Bickle. Mike came to the professional game relatively late. He was working for Co-op Dairies in Plymouth, playing for St Austell in the South-Western League and also for his works team in the Devon Wednesday League. He was scoring shed-loads of goals for St Austell, and eventually came to the attention of Argyle manager Derek Ufton (one of his better decisions, as it turned out). Mike got a run out in the reserves, where he impressed the manager sufficiently to be granted a first-team place. He duly scored on his debut, a 4-1 defeat at Southampton just over a month before his 22nd birthday. He was then left out of the side for the next two League games – although this was in the Christmas/New Year period and he probably had a lot of extra cream to deliver! He was reinstated after a 5-1 defeat at Cardiff on New Year's Day in 1966, and weighed in with two goals on his Home Park debut in a 5-2 victory against Rotherham. The next away game saw Argyle lose 5-1 again, this time at Coventry, with Bickle scoring Argyle's consolation goal. The goals continued to fly in at Argyle's next match, which saw non-League Corby Town visit Home Park in the third round of the FA Cup. Argyle's poor League form went out of the window as the hapless Steelmen were hammered 6-0, with Bickle claiming a hat-trick on his FA Cup debut. A local newspaper announced the arrival of Bix at Argyle with the memorable headline 'Milkman Mike Delivers The Goals Instead Of The Pintas At Home Park' (or something like that). He only missed three more League games that season, and ended up as Argyle's leading scorer (if you include cup games) with an impressive tally of 12 goals in 19 appearances. My first game as an active Argyle fan was a hugely exciting (I expect) 0-0 draw against Huddersfield. I was only to see three more games that season, and they ended in defeats – against Bristol City (0-2), Crystal Palace (1-2 – my first ever Argyle goal, scored by Bickle, of course) and

Southampton, who clinched promotion to the First Division by beating Argyle 3-2 in front of nearly 19,000 at Home Park on the last day of the season, which also happened to be my birthday. I have to be honest and say that I don't really remember very much about those first few games, although there are certain elements, like the smell of stewed tea and cigarette smoke, which will always remain with me. My other early memories of Argyle and of the players are ones of disappointment though (ah, such foresight in one so young). The first was seeing the team run out for the first time. I'd been brought up in an Argyle household and it was drummed into me from an early age that Argyle played in green, black and white – always in that order and NEVER forget the black. So you can imagine my confusion when the team emerged from the tunnel to the strains of 'Semper Fidelis' (and I'll never forget that either) wearing a strip which was almost completely white. Secondly, I remember being disappointed with the way the players celebrated a goal (although I didn't see many that season). I'd already got used to seeing some of the more exuberant celebrations on the telly, by the likes of Denis Law and Ian St John. So I was surprised to see my new heroes greet each goal they scored with a good firm handshake, a manly slap on the back and a leisurely trot back to the halfway line. The following season, with the team back in green (the dreaded white was to return two seasons later), Mike Bickle was to change all that. He'd become a regular first-teamer by now and had claimed the number 9 shirt as his own. He eclipsed his personal best of three with a four-goal haul against Cardiff in a 7-1 Argyle victory in October, and once again ended up as lead-

ing scorer at the end of the season. He celebrated goals the way they were MEANT to be celebrated. I can still see him now, wheeling away after scoring and running to the fans in the Devonport End, arms aloft, teeth out and sideburns flying in the wind (eat your heart out, Trigger – Bix had REAL BIG sidies). To be honest, he didn't always wear the number 9 shirt. There were times when he had to settle for the 8 or the 10, even 11 or 12 on occasions. Like when Bix returned to the side after injury in the 1967/68 season to find the shirt occupied by one of Derek Ufton's desperation signings, the former England international Alan Peacock. That season saw Argyle relegated to the Third Division for the first time in nearly a decade, and much of the damage was done in the opening fourteen games when Bickle was sidelined and Argyle were crying out for a striker. Even the veteran full-back John Sillett was pressed into service for a couple of games. Amongst other square pegs were John Tedesco and Keith Etheridge, who managed one goal between them. Bix continued to ply his trade in the Third Division for the next couple of seasons, and was leading scorer in 1968/69 and 1969/70. There were some memorable goals – another foursome against Torquay in a 6-0 Boxing Day thrashing (when Norman Piper scored direct from a free-kick at the Devonport End, a goal David Beckham would have been proud of) – and a spectacular goal against Swindon, after Argyle had been awarded an indirect free-kick inside the area when the Swindon 'keeper had fallen foul of the 'four steps' rule which was in operation at the time. Swindon, who would be promoted with Watford at the end of the season, had won the League Cup against Arsenal on a Wembley quagmire the previous weekend and had paraded the trophy around the Home Park cinder track before the match. The Argyle players formed a guard of honour to welcome the Swindon team. Billy Bingham had said that he wanted the Argyle players to applaud the Swindon team onto the pitch and then play them off it, which they did – just – as Bickle's goal turned out to be the winner in a 2-1 victory in front of just under 21,000. He was one of Argyle's scorers on the occasion of our first ever appearance on *Match Of The Day* – a surprise 2-0 victory at Luton – in January 1970. It was a bit of a farcical goal in truth, which came about as a result of a horrific mix-up in the Luton defence – so comical that I believe it can be found on one of those Danny Baker footballing gaffes videos. Derek Rickard, another genuine Janner and a 'yardie' to boot, scored the other. Bix also featured in Argyle's debut on the ITV equivalent *The Big Match*, when we drew 1-1 at Aston Villa the following season. He didn't score that day, but he was instrumental in forcing Villa's Charlie Aitken to concede an own goal and he managed to get booked for time-wasting after about 20 minutes. This season (1970/71) was to be Bickle's last full campaign as an Argyle player, and his least productive in terms of goals. He only managed 6 goals in 24 appearances, the last full one of which was in February, after which he was replaced by new signing Jimmy Hinch. He got six more games in at the start of the following season and scored another three goals, taking his total for Argyle to an impressive 74 from 184 starts in all competitions before an ill-fated move to Gillingham, who were managed by a former Argyle colleague, Andy Nelson. While he was at Gillingham, Bickle broke a bone in his neck in a collision with a

team-mate and was forced to retire. He moved back to Plymouth and took a job in the Dockyard as a scaffold rigger. When I was in the yard, I often used to see him and was pleased to see that he was still sporting the luxuriant louse ladders. 'Bickle is the king' the Devonport End used to sing, and he was for a while. He was never the most elegant of players and wasn't blessed with great skill or aerial ability (he was only 5ft 9in) but he knew where the back of the net was and he was always guaranteed to put his heart and soul into the game, a quality which is always recognised and appreciated by fans, especially when a local boy is doing it. He was one of us. We knew it and he knew it – he was our representative on the pitch, and he always gave the impression that he really enjoyed what he did and that he was lucky to be doing it. Most of the denizens of the Devonport End would have loved to have had the chance to play for Argyle, and Bix was almost doing it for us by proxy. There were other local players in the side, but Mike Bickle was the real deal and, as I mentioned earlier, he ended up in the Dockyard – how Janner is that?! Due to his enforced retirement from the game, he was granted a testimonial by Argyle in 1973, when Manchester City brought an almost full-strength side – including Colin Bell, Mike Summerbee and Rodney Marsh – to Home Park. They also included a player who'd played for Argyle in Mike's League debut in 1965 – Tony Book, another Argyle legend. A healthy crowd of over 12,000 turned out for him on his big night, which is all the more impressive when you consider that the match took place only one night after Argyle's final League match of the season, when Rochdale were beaten 3-2 in front of just under 10,000. It was a shame that he couldn't play any part in the match, although he did put in an appearance on the pitch and may have actually done the old ceremonial kick-off thing (I really can't remember). I do remember that he was wearing a three-piece suit with wide lapels and huge flares and an enormous kipper tie with a knot the size of Wales. His hair had grown a bit, which was a surprise – in his Argyle days, he'd always looked slightly out of kilter with the rest of the players of his age, as he'd always had a bit of an Elvis quiff and was probably one of the few people in the country under thirty who used Brylcreem. Most of his contemporaries (like Alan Welsh, Don Hutchins, Neil Hague, Steve Davey and the like) had been experimenting with feather cuts, bubble perms and blow-dried affairs, but Bix seemed to have more in common with some of the older players in the side like Les Latcham and Dave Provan. Perhaps the proximity of Gillingham to London with its trendy boutiques had opened up a whole new world of style and fashion to him – I don't think you could get flares at Sweets or Percy Leskins until about 1980. As magnificent as the suit and tie was, it would have been great to have seen him in an Argyle shirt one more time. Although I wish his career hadn't ended in the tragic way it did, I'm glad I never saw him play for Gillingham. I remember seeing various former 'Gyles play for other clubs, and on a lot of occasions it just didn't look right. One particular instance was the sight of Johnny Hore (another hero of mine whom Tony Waiters once memorably described as resembling Cornish granite in football boots) turning out in the red-and-white stripes of Exeter, which almost turned my stomach, and I'm sure the sight of Bix in anything other than an Argyle shirt would

have been equally unsettling. I would have enjoyed seeing him score in his testimonial and turn to the Devonport End one more time with that toothless grin and his arms raised to the heavens though. As I said, he was one of us and I've always liked to think that when he scored for Gillingham, he celebrated with a good firm handshake and a manly slap on the back from one of his colleagues before trotting back to the centre circle.

Neil Jenkins

It's impossible to pick just one player as there have been so many down the years who have inspired, shown flair, or even simply weighed in with the right goal at the right time. However, for me it's difficult not to be biased towards the time when I started going to watch Argyle in earnest, back in the early 1990s. The start of my regular trips to Home Park coincided with the birth of the Shilton era. There are several players from that time for whom I retain a fondness: Mark Patterson, Mark Edworthy, Paul Dalton, 'Super' Stevie Castle and so on. However, despite the mixed feelings about him among certain contingents of Argyle fans, I've got to admit Trigger is one of my absolute favourites. Say what you will about him, but it cannot be denied that he has played his part by scoring important goals down the years and has been there when it counted. Another favourite from that era is Alan Nicholls – a huge talent who died tragically young. I'm sure he had the ability to achieve great things in his career, had it not been cut so cruelly short. From today's team, I'd say Cocko is the man. He lives and breathes Argyle, defends like his life depends on it and scores goals.

Kevin Hodges' record number of appearances for the Pilgrims will probably never be beaten.

Larrieu is my other current favourite – having seen him take a chest-high tackle in a match at Cheltenham and just get up and get on with it, not to mention the numerous clean sheets he kept to help us win the title, I hope that Romain will remain an Argyle player for many years to come.

Becky Gadd

My favourite Argyle team was the promotion team of 1985/86, and during their successful promotion campaign and the first season they spent in the old Second Division, I thought that Kevin Hodges was always a level above the other players.

When he had the ball, I always felt he could produce a positive move and felt confident that the ball was safe at his feet. I don't think I ever saw him have a bad game! I also have fond memories of Garry Nelson and was able to meet him a few years ago when (amazingly) he turned up at a little local library to promote his book and give a talk. It was gratifying to hear him say that his days at Argyle were probably the best for him in terms of team spirit and enjoying his footie.

Sarah Decent

In the early years, I enjoyed watching Mike Bickle. He was very entertaining and scored some memorable goals, like against Swindon from a close free-kick, the week after they had won the League Cup. He had the 'hero' image to a youngster, and he scored away at Luton in a 2-0 win shown on *Match of the Day*. He also had a punch-up with Fred Molyneux during a game! I liked his swashbuckling style and the fact that he was an ordinary bloke (a milkman). Later, I loved watching Mariner and Rafferty tear teams apart with their incisive running and finishing. Mariner had an eye for goal and was class. I remember his very late goal at Dartford in the FA Cup after we went 2-1 down with 2 minutes left. Rafferty also scored some great goals, including at home against Blackpool in the FA Cup (2-0) from a back-heel flick. Then there was the game at Bournemouth (7-3) in the 1970s, which was memorable for the two tearing into the home defence – we went 5-0 up, then let in three, and finally got two late goals! More recently, I enjoyed Tynan for his instinctive finishing and consistent scoring. The goal of his that stands out was a diving header in the 4-0 win over Bristol City in the promotion year in the 1980s. He had the knack of being in the right place when the cross came in.

Phil Banks

The past player would probably be Alan Nicholls – he always gave 110 per cent and was 100 per cent Green. Shame he never had the chance to shine on the big stage. You always thought that if a fight kicked off, he'd be there in the thick of it. I'll never forget being locked out of Barnet in 1994 (because they'd decided on the morning it was ticket only and told no one), and after pestering the steward out-side the gates to let me in for most of the first half, I eventually got in for the last twenty minutes. I arrived on the away ter-race and within seconds saw Nicholls sent off, for some violent incident outside the box. Poor Dungey arrived on to have to defend a free-kick, which rattled the post. I'll also never forget watching the Argyle fans at Kingstonian singing his name, the Saturday after his bike smash. Of the cur-rent players, it would have to be Trigger. The man's a god. I've never seen him play at less than 110 per cent. His performance in the 2001/02 season at Field Mill was tremendous. You always knew when he left for Southampton that he'd come back. He scored five goals for them in the last few games of that season, almost single-

Mickey Evans – the big target man who has enjoyed two spells with the Greens.

handedly keeping them in the Premiership. For one of them, he knocked himself out against the post! He should be offered the keys to the city, then send them back saying he's not bothered!

Chris Ramsay

Kevin Summerfield was the complete player – and a real class act. Excellent passer, great vision, scored 33 Argyle goals and was a good tackler. He played the game as it should be played – on the ground – and ran the Argyle midfield for five years after signing from Cardiff in 1984 – an integral and highly-skilled part of Dave Smith and Ken Brown's sides. He made a total of 158 appearances for Argyle, with over half of them being in what is now the First Division. His career was virtually ended in 1989 by Graeme Sharp, who broke his leg with a wild challenge in a Cup replay at Everton. When I first moved to Plymouth in 1969, Steve Davey was my first Argyle hero. In his nine-year Argyle career, he was never the 'star' of the team, even though his performances were consistent and he was always one of the most skilful players on show. He was also extremely versatile, as he played equally well at full-back and in midfield as he did in his better-known position of inside forward. Steve's debut for Argyle came in the 3-0 defeat at Blackburn in November 1966, and he scored his first goal for the Greens in his fourth game, a 1-1 draw away to Ipswich later in the same season. By the time I saw him play for the first time – as a substitute for Dave Burnside in the 1-0 home defeat to Brighton in August 1969 – he had already played 70 games (plus 4 as substitute) and

scored 17 goals. Not bad for a player yet to reach his 21st birthday. Davey's scoring prowess slackened off in the early 1970s because new manager Ellis Stuttard decided to play him at right-back, because of injuries. He was unhappy because he saw himself as a forward, but at least he was in the team. Unfortunately, when the regular defenders were available, Steve was out again. Regular forwards at that time – Derek Rickard, Jimmy Hinch and Don Hutchins – were scoring regularly, so he couldn't get a game up front either. This changed during 1972/73 when he fought his way back into the team in his favoured position up front. He didn't let anyone down either, with 9 goals in only 17 appearances, including a hot spell of 5 in 3 games in early February. The change in Davey's fortunes seemed to arrive with the appointment of Tony Waiters as manager. Waiters appeared to be the only boss who appreciated Davey's particular skills and contribution to the team. This bore fruit with Davey's best Argyle season in 1973/74, when he was paired with new non-League signing Paul Mariner in a potent strike force. Davey was a virtual ever-present in the team, and although Mariner scored more League goals, Davey came out on top overall with his contribution in the League Cup, where he scored 7 times in 6 ties. In all, he scored 19 goals in 51 games, compared to Mariner's 17 in 50. It was the League Cup matches that I personally remember Steve best for. I was lucky enough to see 4 of the 6 ties, and Davey scored in all of them. The 2-0 win at Fourth Division Torquay in the first round was fairly routine, with Davey scoring both. Argyle annihilated Second Division Portsmouth 4-0 at Home Park in the second round, with Davey again scoring twice. Then came three consecutive games away from home against First Division opposition. Each time, Argyle were given no chance, but each time they defied the odds to go through. I missed the games at Burnley (who were third), which we won 2-1, and QPR (who were second) which we 3-0, but was lucky enough to get to St Andrews on 19 December 1973 to see Steve Davey score his greatest goal for Argyle – which also proved to be the winner. Alan Walsh had equalised Birmingham's early lead in the 35th minute. A couple of minutes later, Argyle were in front. Jim Furnell launched a long kick up field; Davey chased it down and hit a spectacular 30-yard shot past the helpless Birmingham 'keeper. Route one at its best! Argyle never looked like surrendering the lead and we were in the semi-final. The first leg was played on a Wednesday afternoon because of the threat of power cuts. Manchester City were lucky to escape from Home Park with a 1-1 draw. Davey scored another excellent goal when he turned Scottish international Willie Donachie on the edge of the penalty area, and flashed the ball past McCrae in the Devonport End goal. Davey later fractured his collarbone going for a second and missed the second leg, which Argyle lost 2-0. The incident that effectively cost Davey his Argyle career, happened on Sunday 10 March – 'Black Sunday' – at Port Vale. Davey scored in Argyle's 2-1 defeat, but was also sent off, along with Bobby Saxton and Dave Provan. During his suspension, Tony Waiters brought in another striker – Billy Rafferty – with the intention of using a three-man strike force of Mariner, Rafferty and Davey. However, at the start of 1974/75, Davey hadn't scored in the first 6 games. Waiters decided to change things

and have a 4-4-2 formation with two wide players, with Rafferty and Mariner as the strike force. The decision was justified, as Argyle were promoted and the Mariner/ Rafferty partnership was prolific. Steve Davey played in the Combination League for the rest of the season and, at the end of it, was sold to Hereford. He scored 18 goals in his first season at Edgar Street as Hereford won the Third Division Championship. However, they went into freefall and were relegated two years on the trot to end up in the Fourth Division. Davey joined Portsmouth and played for them for three years. He then turned down a move to Wimbledon and joined Exeter instead. It was a sad end to a career of much promise, but I will always remember the contribution he made to Argyle fortunes in 1973/74, and the joy he gave me personally. Steve Davey will always be one of my all-time Argyle heroes.

Steve Nicholson

The best player for me has to be the great Tommy Tynan, firstly for becoming the hero that attracted me to Argyle in the early Eighties – particularly the '84 Cup run – and secondly for proving that heroes can also be genuine, nice, down-to-earth people. Two friends and I found his address in the school registers (his daughter attended the same school, Southway) and then walked the five miles to his house in order to get his autograph. The three-hour wait outside his house to pluck up the courage to knock on the door was worth it, as we were invited in by the man himself. He provided the requested autographs, along with a stack of photographs, and to top it off, he promised to get us tickets for

65

the FA Cup final if Argyle could beat Watford in the semi-final the following week. The final never occurred, but his promise to three 14-year-olds will remain eternally etched in my Argyle memory banks.

Michael Kitteridge

I've had many favourite players in the years I've been supporting Argyle, but my favourite two, apart from the obvious (Tynan and Hodges) were Paul Dalton and Martin Barlow. Dalton was always full of running, taking on defenders and never afraid to have a crack at goal. Barlow, on the other hand, was a busy midfielder, who never gave up and strung excellent passes around the field.

Benjie Ward

Nobody can beat the Mariner/Rafferty combination. It was just pure magic to watch and the greatest upset to me when Waiters sold Rafferty in a vain attempt to hang on to Mariner.

Steve Barrie

Tommy Tynan was a legend and was one of the reasons I voted to move to Plymouth in 1989 when my family relocated from Berkshire. I saw him in his final Argyle season. Paul Dalton was probably the best winger I have ever seen at Argyle. His dribbling, crossing and shooting were brilliant, and I got a real thrill from watching him run down that left wing, right in front of where I stood on the Mayflower. I have

a signed picture of Dalton on my office wall, which will always have pride of place.

Mark Williams

As I enter my thirteenth season as an Argyle fan, I initially considered the task of choosing a single favourite player to be a difficult one. It wasn't until I was having this discussion with a fellow Argyle fan that I realised there is a clear choice after all: the enigma that is Paul Dalton. Right from his arrival at Home Park, he proved to possess the quality which had previously been lacking in our wingers. His skilful forays down the wing shone a ray of hope into otherwise dreary games. His greatest performance for us must surely have been the game away at Hartlepool, where his fantastic afternoon was capped with a dazzling run that appeared to see him take on, and beat, every member of the Hartlepool team, before planting the ball firmly in the net – Dalton at his best! As a fan watching from the terraces with my brother Mark, we would sometimes lose patience with the pace of a game. At this stage, one would turn to the other and say 'Oh, just give it to Dalton for God's sake!' We both knew that he had the ability to turn a game on his own. My lingering memory of Paul Dalton can be summed up in another quote from the days of watching Argyle with Mark. During an infamous Dalton assault down the opposing wing, my brother quoted the wonderful Blackadder series, to sum up that 'he twists and turns like a twisty turny thing!' What more can I say?!

Clare Williams

5 Memorable goals

Fred Binney's goal at Portsmouth in the 5-1 away win in 1978. A Pompey defender, near the corner flag, took a throw-in back to his own 'keeper, who came running out to collect it and slipped on his backside. The ball rolled towards the net and Fred tapped it in on the line. Laugh?

Malcolm Sheryn

The best goal I've seen was a Paul Wotton screamer against Brighton in the Auto Windscreens Trophy in 1994. It's a shame there were less than a thousand at Home Park to witness it, which is why it is more memorable.

Smudja (Richard Smith)

Most bizarre goal: Kevin Nugent, against Reading, in the 3-1 home win in March 1994 – Shaka Hislop had twice poorly kicked the ball out, and the third time it hit Kev on the back and he turned round and scored. Best goal: a Dave Kemp flicked diving header against Carlisle in a 4-2 home win in November 1979 – it typified the sheer class of the man as a striker. Any goal by Tommy Tynan (my eyes mist up at the thought of him!) but THE ONE against WBA in the fifth round of THAT RUN was special. A John Delve 30-yarder against

Bury in the promotion season (1974/75), was so special that, again, Brian Moore on *The Big Match* the following week showed it after someone had written in to request it (wonderful shaky 35mm pictures from Westward and Chris Fear's commentary). Another great one was a Paul Mariner header against Brighton on Good Friday 1975, which I swear was from the very edge of the area. Finally 'Sabella' Summerfield's winning goal in a 2-1 result at Ipswich in 1988 is definitively my all-time Argyle great goal (for sheer quality, if not significance). Another bizarre goal is the one scored by a Reading defender in August 1986 in a 1-0 win for Plymouth at Elm Park. It happened right on the stroke of half-time and it turned out to be the winner. The bizarre thing about it was that Dave Smith, the manager at the time, had left for the dressing room a few seconds earlier and didn't see it. Moreover, no mention was apparently made of it at half-time. So Smithy claimed that when the game finished, he thought it was a 0-0 draw, and it wasn't until they were back in the dressing room that he found out Argyle had not only won, but were top of the League!

Andy Milligan

The goal I remember is one against us! I've only ever been to Hartlepool once – and I got lucky when I witnessed Argyle's record-equalling 8-1 victory there. However, my recollection above all other is the sheer frustration, annoyance and downright anger of Argyle's young and extremely promising goalkeeper, Alan Nicholls, when the defence did not afford him appropriate cover, and Hartlepool scored their consolation goal. He went absolutely ballistic and it clearly illustrated the level of pride and professionalism that he personally felt at having been beaten. Sadly, he was to lose his life a little later in a tragic motorcycle accident. He had all the makings of a top 'keeper, and who knows, he may well have graced the field for a Premiership club.

Bob Gelder

The best goal, in my opinion, was scored by Paul Dalton *v.* Barnsley in the FA Cup in 1994. Marshall's was also fantastic (scored from practically on the touchline), but Dalton seemed to glide past all the defenders effortlessly. He was a quality player. Other goals include the Barlow 'van Basten' effort and McGregor's strike to complete his hat-trick *v.* Barnet. Most bizarre goals – I remember a Crewe defender once scored an own goal with a header from outside the penalty area, a notable achievement! Also McCarthy's away to Cheltenham a couple of seasons back – the most blatant foul on the 'keeper AND handball I've ever seen! That made it 4-1, if I remember rightly, greeted with sarcastic applause!

Andrew Smith

The funniest goal has got to be Kevin Jobling for Grimsby at Blundell Park. It

was the season before we went down under Kemp, I think. Dave Walter (possibly the most famous sheep-farming goalkeeper) came out to smother a shot and spilt it about 12 yards out. Jobling then took it round Walter, who was still grounded, but doing some strange breakdance move on the floor in an effort to get to the ball. Obviously, he didn't get to the ball, and as it rolled into the net, Walter did a strange tuck jump into the goal. Just too bizarre. The most significant goal? Marino Keith's goal at Carlisle. It was at that moment that I finally believed that we would be Champions. The best? Wotton's free-kick against Preston a few years back. If the net hadn't been there, the ball would have been on its way to Cornwall. I remember that Tepi Moilanen only started to dive for the top corner when the ball was in the back of the net.

Joe Fielder

As a kid, I wanted to be the next John S. Williams and shoot goals from 30 yards at will. His were always memorable.

Keith Whitfield

Steve Davey's winner against Birmingham at St Andrews in the 1973/74 League Cup quarter-final, when he volleyed the ball past Dave Latchford from about 40 yards, was 'a bit special' (as Big Ron might say). I was one of the fortunate few Argyle fans to see this one as the game was played on a Wednesday afternoon during the energy strikes and power cuts of the Winter of Discontent. Westward TV showed highlights of the game the following day. Their camerawork was always a little on the amateurish side; you would often see coverage of an Argyle match where you would see a player shoot and the next shot would be the 'keeper picking the ball out of the net. So it was surprising when intrepid announcer Don Arnold said something like 'Unfortunately, our cameras missed Steve Davey's winner, but the boys in the backroom have come up with something'. We sat waiting for the slow-mo replay, but all we got was someone with a blackboard and chalk describing the goal to us. The most photogenic must surely be wee Hughie Reed's diving header in another Boxing Day fixture against Torquay. A couple more contenders both involve Brentford. The first was in 1969/70, when the ball went into the Argyle goal through a gap in the side netting. The Argyle and Brentford players were all preparing for a

goal kick when the referee decided to award a goal to Brentford. The goal turned out to be the only one of the game. Argyle got their revenge in a 2-1 FA Cup win against the Bees in 1973/74 when, with the score at 1-1 and only a few minutes left, Stewart Houston executed the perfect lob over the 'keeper from about 30 yards out. Unfortunately for Houston, it was over his own 'keeper and Argyle went through.

Neil Jenkins

The most bizarre, and certainly the most significant in the wider footballing sense, was surely Jimmy Glass's 95th-minute thump to keep Carlisle in the League. A goal against is never usually a momentous occasion, but only a truly bitter and

Unbelievable scenes as Argyle somehow allow goalkeeper Jimmy Glass to score to save Carlisle from relegation.

Joyous scenes at Brunton Park, as the fans celebrate Carlisle's dramatic last-minute escape.

twisted Argyle fan would wish to forget our part in that small moment of history. The best goal I ever saw was by Kevin Summerfield at Portman Road in February 1988. Nicky Law had already equalised with a screamer from way out, which had us all stunned – television later ruined it by showing it was more likely a mis-hit cross! In the second half, playing towards the away end, Summers picked up the ball well inside our half. There then followed the kind of mazy run that's seen Maradona and John Barnes hailed as gods. Three despairing Ipswich defenders were shrugged off and, eclipsing the deities, Summers finished by going outside the last defender and smacking a screamer into the opposite corner of the net. Delirium ensued – it turned out to be the winner too. Funnily enough, it's Summers again who scored my most memorable Argyle goal. Away to Pompey on Easter Monday 1987, Argyle were hanging on to a play-off spot for the top division, Pompey were doing better and boasting a year-long unbeaten home record too. 0-0 and well into the second half, Summers comes off the bench and, within what seemed like seconds, had anticipated a typically clogger-like back pass from future Exeter boss Noel Blake, latched onto it and blasted it past Alan Knight. Again, it was right in front of the Argyle fans, again delirium ensued, and again it turned out to be the winner.

Richard Smith

The best goal recently has got to be Marino Keith's looping shot over Exeter's 'keeper to seal the Devon derby in the

2001/02 season at Nou Home Park. The best goal from the past is John Uzzell's 45-yarder from the left wing, which looped over the Forest 'keeper during his testimonial match. The funniest goal was Owen Pickard's only goal for Argyle (to my knowledge) at Home Park – off the back of his shoulder. He went to power it home, but it hit his shoulder and literally fell over the line with no force. Made I laugh.

Andy Laidlaw

The best goal I can remember is in the FA Cup v. Barnsley at Home Park, scored by Dwight Marshall. The game finished 2-2, and the goal was typical of that season's team under Shilton: a free-flowing move, involving lots of passes starting from our own box. Dwight beat a couple of defenders out wide right, cut inside and finished. I'd have been 14 or 15 at the time, so perhaps it might not have been the greatest goal of all time, but it sure stuck in my mind. Typically, we lost the replay 2-0.

Jon Lambert

I have hated every goal scored against Argyle – except one. The world's greatest player, appearing on the hallowed turf and playing against my team. Pelé may have only tucked away a penalty, but it's a memory that will live with me forever. But Mike Dowling did his best to steal the headlines with a screamer. It came as no surprise to me, as I had seen him have a number of long-range efforts for the reserves, but it must have been a special moment for him to deliver one of his best against Santos. One of the best Argyle

goals from the past for me was Darren Rowbotham's at Highbury – the only bright spot of a cup drubbing, but a goal of sheer class.

Gordon Sparks

The best goal I've ever seen at Home Park was Barlow's van Basten effort from the Sleepers Corner, which I can still see now, even though the details of the game have long since faded from my memory. There must be something about that corner as another favourite goal was Adrian Littlejohn's escape from two markers down there, followed by a break along the byline and a lethal dispatch across the 'keeper. The funniest? Step forward McCarthy's arse at Southend. It's a shame that someone who played at the highest level should be remembered by Argyle fans for his backside and elbows. As for significant goals, there is Garry Nelson's run from the halfway line and rocket into the top corner against Bristol City in '86, which secured Argyle's spot in the old Second Division. Little did I know at the time that my cancelled trip to Darlington would lead to a sixteen-year wait to visit there for another glorious four-goal display in an equally significant game.

Stuart Caskey

The best has to be Mike Dowling's goal against Santos: a superb strike from just inside the Santos half. Argyle, of course, won 3-2. The most significant has to be Reilly's goal against Argyle in the FA Cup semi-final against Watford. Without it, the game would surely have gone into extra time and Argyle would have been odds on to win the tie and get through to the final. The most bizarre has to be an own goal scored by a Blackpool defender at Home Park. The ball hit the post and came out, but the defender thought it had gone in and simply hit the ball into the net in disgust. Thank you, 1-0 to Argyle.

Keef Newham

Garry Nelson v. Bristol City, 29 April 1986. In the match with Bristol City, which saw Argyle clinch promotion to the Second Division, this was the goal that settled the team just after half-time. A pass out of defence to Tommy Tynan on the halfway line, followed by a deft flick from Tynan into Garry Nelson's path, who took the ball on and smashed an unstoppable drive over Waugh in the City goal. Gary Lineker scored a similar goal around the same time and the press raved about it for months. I remember a goal scored by Johnny Hore at Home Park against Rochdale in the last game of the 1972/73 season. Well, to say I remember the goal would be stretching the truth a little – what I remember is the beaming smile across Hore's face after he buried the ball into the Devonport End net. It was also the significance of the goal that I remember. It was the days of the short-lived 'Watney Cup'. Two teams from each division qualified – the top two scoring teams who weren't promoted, relegated or European qualifiers. The two Third Division teams played at home to the two from the First Division and the two from

the Fourth at home to the Second Division qualifiers. Going into the last match of the season, Argyle needed two goals to gain their place. Argyle were confident, having already beaten Rochdale 6-0 away. They raced into a 3-0 lead by half-time, with two from Neil Hague, and eventually won 3-2, but it was Hore's goal that was the vital second. The result gave us a home tie with Stoke City (how the mighty have fallen). We lost 1-0!

Steve Nicholson

For me, one of the best goals was Hughie Reed's diving header against Torquay on Boxing Day, 1971. I was in the Devonport End, right behind the goal – I can see it now. Most significant was Tommy Tynan against WBA in the FA Cup in 1984. I flew all the way from Germany to see that one! Thanks, Tommy.

Keith Frood

As mentioned – and how could I forget? – a goalkeeper scoring in the 95th minute to keep his club in the League – and save a few Argyle fans lives at the same time, as a few of those Carlisle boys didn't take kindly to their perilous position. The stewards thought a small piece of netting was good enough to keep them away while they went for some tea and biscuits with ten minutes to go.

Neil Carhart

6 Memorable trips

Losing 3-0 away at Sheffield Wednesday in the FA Cup in 1968. On the Pilgrim Express (Argyle's own chartered train) returning from Hillsborough in a freezing January, the buffet had run out of everything. As a youngster who had had a few (not too many) cans of Pale Ale, my mouth was desperate for refreshment. The train stopped at Bristol Temple Meads around midnight, and loads of fans rushed out to the station buffet to grab what they could. The queue was uncomfortably long, but I was desperate. The train started going as I was getting served, I dashed after the train, my friends had the door open, but a policeman stopped me from jumping on it. Everything was on that train, including my coat. Three of us had to wait for the mail train at five-thirty on Sunday morning to get back to Plymouth. On arrival, I had a twelve-mile walk home. That was a miserable and cold night on a railway station platform! Another memorable journey was to Hereford, circa December/January 1977. I drove from Plymouth through snow and ice, and arrived in Hereford at 6 p.m. Sitting in a café, I saw the bloke opposite had a newspaper. The back page read 'United game off.' Hereford ... City? County? Athletic? Rangers? Bollocks – it's United! Playing Blackpool away in 1996 (a 2-2 draw), Bloomfield Road was so windy, I genuinely feared for our safety. The galvanised cladding in the terracing seemed to be hanging on by the last bolt. I spent most of the time looking up and over my shoulder. It was frightening.

Malcolm Sheryn

A Wednesday night game away at Brighton in March 1994 ranks among the most exhausting and depressing trips ever. I drove up from St Austell to Plymouth and caught the supporters' coach in the early afternoon. The match saw us battle for what seemed a respectable draw. Then, in the last two minutes, Steve Castle was sent off and Paul Dickov scored an outrageous volleyed winner from outside the area for Brighton. Our promotion hopes had taken a hit, and I was faced with many dark hours on the coach and a drive through Cornwall. I got to bed at 4.30 a.m. and was up for work three hours later. To say I was in a foul mood that day at work would be an understatement. The abortive trip to Darlington in March 2002 was difficult, memorable and bizarre. We left London and the south in relative sunshine and clear skies. As is standard practice, once we eased north of Nottinghamshire, the clouds of the grim north exerted their grip. We were aware of wet weather being forecast for the north, and so rang Darlington FC for an update at about 10.30 a.m. We were reassured that no inspections were planned, no problems foreseen. The weather on the M1 got worse, going from drizzle to more persistent rain. Nothing to worry about. Nevertheless, we rang again an hour after our first attempt. We received the same reply of confidence. About 20 miles or so from Darlington, the rain turned to snow, and I don't mean gradual snow via sleet and showers. I mean blizzards. And it was settling. We called the club again at 12.30 p.m. The woman at Darlington assured us there was no danger of the game being called off, no inspection was planned and generally all was well. We parked up in the snowscape of Darlington town centre in March and made for the pub. It was filling up with plenty of Plymouth fans from far and wide. At 1.10 p.m., the game was called off because of a waterlogged pitch. Having subsequently seen pictures of the pitch that morning, I was not surprised. So we all had a few drinks and a grumble, and headed back on the motorway. Of course, half-an-hour out of Darlington and the snow disappeared. Games across the country continued outside our north-eastern bubble, while we were faced with a wasted day and a re-arranged midweek trip. We had our revenge as the fixture saw Argyle win the Division Three Championship. A less palatable memory is the trip to Peterborough in September 1998. It was a sunny, warm day. There were four of us in the car as we left north London. I had been to a party the night before and was suffering from a searing hangover. I felt I had it under control, and was looking forward to some fresh air sorting me out. However, there are a lot of roundabouts on the A1 to Peterborough. After several of these, my insides suddenly decided they wanted to be on the outside,

and we couldn't stop the car in time. I painted myself, the inside of the car, and the roadside with the previous night's offerings. The other two passengers legged it in fear of the smell setting them off and the driver was not surprisingly worried about his car. I knelt at the roadside in a praying position. We used the facilities at a car showroom down the road and I had to ditch a t-shirt altogether. The car smelled unpleasant to say the least. Once in Peterborough, bar staff and various supporters were informed of my plight and took full advantage of the taunting opportunities. Thankfully, Plymouth won the game 2-0. Every time I pass that spot on the A1, I wince. And I am eternally sorry to Jan, Dale and Kevin for making it a day to remember.

Toby Jones

I can remember a midweek trip away to Mansfield in the late 1970s or early '80s. Fifteen of us, Dem'port End regulars, had booked a minibus in advance. Unfortunately, the normal seated bus was not available, and the hire company provided a large van as a replacement, the seating being two wooden benches on each side of the van. So every time we went around a corner, the human occupants on one side of the van would dive head first at the occupants on the other side. This caused great hilarity, which made the journey up just about bearable. Unfortunately, the buuys got stuffed 5-0 by the Stags, whose manager at the time was a certain future 'Ciderman'. Also, we got a good soaking on the open away terrace, as the heavens opened. It was so dire that we all left early to get more beer in to prepare us mentally for the long trek home. The journey home was a nightmare. Everybody gave up on the benches and tried to sleep on the van floor. Unfortunately, the van didn't seem to have any suspension, and every bump sent a shudder through my body, so sleep was impossible. When we finally arrived back in Plymouth at about four or five in the morning, it was not a pretty sight. 'Walking death' would be a good description. I have never ached so much in my life. Mind you, I was young in those days and was able to recover and set off for work at 6.30 a.m. for a day's skiving in Dem'port Dockyard. Truly an away trip from hell.

Peter Colbourne

This has got to be the postponement away to Notts County, just after Christmas in 1998. It was very cold and there was a big freeze on across the country. When we left Plymouth to drive up to County, we phoned them to check if the game was on – the answer was yes, and there was no plan for an inspection. To be on the safe side, we decided to phone again at about 11.30 a.m. Again, we were told: 'yes, the game is in no doubt'. We were very pleased with this and looking forward to the game. We arrived at the ground at 1.15 p.m., just as it was announced on Radio 5 that the game was off. How we felt, I just cannot express. Apparently, the ref. felt the pitch may freeze over at about 4.30 p.m., so called it off. It really was infuriating. We ended up watching Coventry v. Middlesbrough. Boring … Another nightmare journey was away to Scarborough on a Tuesday night when Kevin Hodges was the manager. Anyway,

we got to the game OK, but after the game, we were driving out on the only main road away from Scarborough at about 10.15 p.m. when we hit a traffic jam. The road was blocked by a very nasty accident. At 1.30 a.m., we were still trying to get through. We eventually got back to Plymouth at 6.30 in the morning. I was driving and was in work at 8 a.m. that Wednesday. Oh, and we lost as well.

Keef Newham

One memorable trip to an Argyle match was the away fixture against Rotherham in 1992/93. I can't tell you anything about the game, because I did not see a ball kicked. We arrived in good time for the game and headed for the pub for a few pre-match bevvies. As we left the pub, Dave, the driver, came towards us and said that the car had been stolen. We thought he was joking – unfortunately, he wasn't. The first problem – for me anyway – was that I am diabetic and my insulin was in the car. After reporting the situation to the police, the other three headed for Millmoor, while Dave and I headed for the local hospital. The closest we got to the match was when one of the Rotherham players was brought in with a head injury. Eventually, I was supplied with some insulin and we headed back to Millmoor – just in time for the final whistle. What to do next? None of us had any money for train fares. Eventually, I decided to take the bull by the horns, and headed for the area for officials only at the ground. I thought I could ask the club to borrow some money to get us back to Bristol. Dan McCauley would have none of it. Instead, he offered us a lift home on the team coach! Peter

Shilton actually said 'no', but McCauley insisted, so there we were – five Argyle fans on the team bus. The players and officials on the coach treated us all very well, we were fed and watered and we were met at Gordano Services by Diane's dad, who took us the rest of the way home. *Buffy the Vampire Slayer* will always remind me of what started out as a disaster and ended up being one of the best days of my whole life. Oh, and Argyle drew the match 2-2.

Steve Nicholson

At the age of 15, I had the worst journey of my life on the way back from seeing Argyle hammer Hartlepool 8-1 in 1994. At a train change in Darlington, I missed the connection. I had no money left, and it was the last train down south that evening. Thankfully, after hours of waiting, I managed to talk the National Express coach driver into giving me a lift to Heathrow airport. My dad had to come and pick me up at about half-past five in the morning. He was not best pleased, and I was banned from making my own way to Burnley for the first leg of the play-offs.

Sam Fleet

Argyle were in Sweden for a pre-season tour in July 1990, and an assorted collection of PASALBs travelled by various routes to there in search of blondes, 'cheap' beer and encouragement for the forthcoming season – sadly, only one of these was to be found in plentiful supply. The advance guard of Blackler, Coker, Metcalf and Scowcroft met at the

Heathrow terminal one bar on 19 July and, after some delay, we downed our final drink on English soil for a week. We arrived on time at Gothenburg and had our first sighting of a blonde Swede – on the Hertz car rental desk. Rupert negotiated a generous rate, and hired a Volvo 740 as well, and then we set off for town (after a minor hiccup trying to work out how to get the car in gear). Our first impression of Sweden was how slow the speed limit is – 55mph on motorways. Rupert soon decided to ignore that! After finding our hotel and depositing the car, we started the most difficult part of the tour – hunt a pub! On the first night, we got lucky – a real pub, subdued lighting and a few hardened drunks. PASALB were naturally at home, although at £4 a drink, no one rushed to buy a round! The serious business started on Saturday 21st. We had a pleasant day driving along the coast before arriving at Tvaaker an hour before kick-off. The game was in a public park, and the first person we saw was Lewis Ridge – well, we couldn't have a first-team game without Lewis. Another PASALB, Steve Nicholson, and his father, Joe, had also made it. David Kemp came over to chat to us. Some Arsenal fans were also there, and they gave Rhys a great reception. The match started in front of about 300 fans in beautiful sunshine. Tony took about 90 seconds to question the officials' eyesight, and the local team took only a minute longer to expose Argyle's rustiness at the back and take the lead. Within half an hour they'd gone 2-0 up, and things looked bleak. A smartly-worked goal from King just before half-time and an improved second-half performance, with further goals from King and Byrne, gave the Greens a victory. We stayed that night in

Halmstad, where the team was based. As usual, bars were few and far between. There were queues to get into the two main bars, and we met some of the players also looking for an empty bar. As usual, PASALB instincts did not let us down and we found a superb bar with a gorgeous blonde barmaid, as well as a couple of genuine Swedish drunks – complete with beer guts – a rare sighting of this endangered species! The next day was a quiet one, spent travelling to Mälmo. We had an enjoyable lunch at a small fishing port before reaching our destination. There, we met more PASALBs, Keith Bernhardt and Alistair Black, before going off to watch Mälmo play Osters in a Swedish League game, which finished 1-1 and was largely a bore. The Argyle players were even more unfortunate, seeing a goal-less game at Halmstad. The final PASALB joined our befuddled group – the almost legendary Steve Magner. Trelleborg was next on the itinerary – an industrial port on Sweden's south coast. There's not much to say about the place or the game, a 0-0 draw. Dreadful probably sums both up. The local paper likened Argyle's performance to that of a 'suppository'! Argyle had three players out with injury – maybe some PASALBs could have done better. We met 'the only fan from Plymouth', Andy Moles, who got a lot of publicity in the *Herald*, but we had already met Joe Nicholson. 25 July saw the penultimate day of the tour and Argyle faced what, on paper, was their hardest match – against Lund. We arrived in Lund after a short tour of a nature reserve to find Messrs Black and Magner flagrantly breaking the law! Their crime was drinking cans of beer on a bench in the city square. (Un)fortunately, they weren't apprehended – you can never find

a policeman when you want one – even in Sweden. Argyle played well, which was a welcome surprise. Owen Pickard scored an easy hat-trick and the lads won 3-1. Lund, who included a former Swedish international, Thomas Sjoberg, were very poor, but at least we had started to look like a team. The first half was played in heavy rain, and it was so dark we could hardly see the pitch. During the game, we befriended some Mälmo supporters and gave them copies of *Pasty News*. Their knowledge of English football was amazing, although they were disappointed to learn that Tommy Tynan had left us. We finished our last night spending all our remaining beer money and staggered home at 2 a.m.

John Coker

The most difficult journey to an Argyle match was the FA Cup quarter-final replay with Derby County in 1984. Having been picked up in Richmond by Peter Hake at 2 p.m., we proceeded along the M1 to Dunstable, where we were to collect another friend of Peter's on our way to the Baseball Ground. On arrival in Dunstable, Peter, to our horror, suddenly announced that he was having trouble with the car, and we promptly ground to a halt. The initial reaction was devastation. Three-and-a-half hours away from the kick-off of one of Argyle's most important matches in history, having already made the trip to Plymouth for the home game, the world seemed almost at an end. However, in hindsight, two things were to our advantage in this dire situation. Firstly, we broke down in the town and not on the motorway, and secondly it was still before 5.30 p.m., so we had a chance. Some quick thinking by Peter resulted in us managing to secure a hire car to take us the rest of the way, so after a short delay, we picked up Peter's friend and proceeded happily up the M1, hoping to get to Derby in time for kick-off. We got to Derby around half-an-hour before kick-off, and managed to park the car relatively close to the ground. With excitement in our stride, we walked briskly to the ground and took up our position in the away end to enjoy the pre-match atmosphere, when suddenly Peter shouts out: 'Oh shit, I've lost the car keys.' Following his initial panic, Peter casts his mind back over events and realises he may have left them in the car door. The two of us rapidly leave the ground and proceed at full pelt back to the car, where the four doors are vacant of any protruding key. Then we look at the car boot, where gleaming in the street lighting is a silver key. Hallelujah! We race back to the ground just in time for kick-off and sing heartily with the rest of the Greens to cheer Argyle on to a famous victory. What a night!

Tim Wesley

We were playing Derby County on Saturday and it was repeatedly announced that the match would not be off, even though snow was forecast, due to the Baseball Ground having undersoil heating. So we set off early in our Peugeot 205 GTi from Penzance – Oscar, Steve and myself. The weather gradually got worse but still, it was on! Eventually, we got to Derby's outskirts and decided some fish and chips would be in order, so we stopped. Just as we got back into the car, it was announced on the radio the match was off due to the fact that the ref. could

not see both ends from the centre spot, thanks to the fog. So we turned round and started back down the motorway, which by now was strewn with abandoned cars. There was a massive pile-up, with cars from behind us piling into the cars beside us – even a Roller had been abandoned. Anyway, we were lucky and carried on, eventually stopping at a service station. Unfortunately, we clipped the kerb on the way into the service station and burst a tyre. We waited for the RAC, but as we were about to leave the restaurant area, we bumped into Peter Bloom, the chairman, who asked us where we had travelled from. We said 'Penzance'. He retorted 'You must be mad!' We went to the rearranged game on a Tuesday night and stood next to Cyril Regis, who was watching his relation, David Regis.

Timothy Smart

I suppose the longest distance I have travelled to watch Argyle was on the pre-season tour of Sweden in 1990. I was determined to get there, and I talked my dad into coming too. Having discovered that Sweden was prohibitively expensive, I booked us flights to and accommodation in Copenhagen. From there, we could 'easily' get to the three matches in the Mälmo area – a short boat trip from Copenhagen. Day one almost put us off for the whole week. The train from Copenhagen boarded the boat and then headed north. The nearest station to Tvaakker was Varberg – unfortunately, this meant a £30 taxi ride each way to see the match! Worth it though, as Argyle came back from 2-0 down to win 3-2. The next match was much easier to get to, as we got the boat to Mälmo and the bus to Trelleborg. We had a chat with David Kemp in the town before watching a fairly poor match, which ended 0-0. The final game was in Lund – a suburb of Mälmo and again easy to find. It was Argyle's best performance of the tour – and there was an easy hat-trick for Owen Pickard, as we won 3-1. We spent a week in Sweden, travelling to Argyle by plane, boat, train and bus for a total cost of about £350 – which was a lot in 1990. I remember a fantastic comment from a local in Dorking the day Argyle played there in the FA Cup under Peter Shilton. The 'ex-wing commander' type had obviously read their local paper, in which the game was referred to as 'Dorking's Cup Final'. As we got out of the car in a pretty packed central car park, he said: 'Don't think I'll bother – I forgot about the bally cup final'. Classic. Another memorable journey was when I returned to Bristol after losing 4-0 to Everton in the FA Cup replay. In those days, I used to ride my motorcycle to Michael Wood service station and pick up the supporters' coach from Plymouth. I hadn't passed my motorbike test, but I took a calculated risk and drove the half-mile to the service station from the nearest motorway exit. (This info. will be important later.) When I was dropped off – well after midnight – I got on the bike and headed home. Unfortunately, I was headed off at the pass by the local plod: 'Can I see your licence please, sir?' Provisional only! 'Where have you been?' 'Everton, to watch Plymouth Argyle play.' 'Not your night, is it?' Three points on a provisional licence and a £40 fine!

Steve Nicholson

In the promotion season (1974/75), during the winter, I went to the Tuesday evening match at Huddersfield. I was living in Leicestershire at the time, so caught the train up. We won the match 2-0 (Mariner and Rafferty) in front of about 1,900 spectators. There were constant snow showers throughout the match and it was bitterly cold. On my return journey, I managed to get the last train from Leeds to Derby and then had to hitch-hike from there. I got back at about 4.30 in the morning, frozen stiff, but happy!

Keith Roe

I remember hitching from Essex University to Dartford for the FA Cup match, which we won 3-2. I had very long hair and a dirty old greatcoat and set off about 9 a.m. I would never have picked me up, but I made it through the Dartford tunnel after about four lifts. I took the train back and was badly scared by rather unhappy Dartford fans when walking from the ground to the station. The trip down from North Devon to Plymouth to see the League Cup semi-final versus Man City was also eventful. We took the day off school and the weather was awful. We had to divert around a fallen tree just outside Bideford and had to miss Hatherleigh, because the road was closed due to flooding, but we got there.

Peter Hake

I travelled to see Argyle at Watford with a Newcastle-supporting mate (very deaf, Polish wife) and my dad. This was the year we ended up relegated from the Second to the Second, and Newcastle, who'd been vying for third bottom with us all season, stayed up. My Newcastle mate drove and I directed. After four times round the Watford one-way system, we found the pub he had picked out in his out-of-date *Good Beer Guide*. We parked up opposite, and my mate opened the boot, so that he could munch a few Polish garlic sausages before we went in for a pint, with my dad complaining bitterly about the smell. We went into the pub and swiftly realised that we were probably the only ones in there not to have spent some time detained at Her Majesty's pleasure. We attempted to buy some cigarettes, which everyone enjoyed, as I was the only one in there who didn't know that first the drawer sticks, and then it comes out completely (empty) and you bang your head on the wall behind. I asked the barman for my money back, got it, and a queue swiftly formed of others with the same complaint. We had by then ordered some food. They shouted when it was ready, and some regular complained that he had ordered that and why were we being served first? My dad swiftly explained that it was because he wasn't pretty enough. We got away with it, but left shortly after. We saw the game – 0-0 or 0-1 – I don't really remember. Then on the way home, we heard that King Kevin had arrived at Newcastle and they'd beaten Bristol City 3-0. My Newcastle mate was inconsolable that we hadn't gone there instead.

Mike S.

The train journey to Darlo in the Championship season, the first time around, with 'Loud' and others, feeling like death, due to the 'flu. We got to the meeting pub, it was snowing, and I discovered that we were going to be on an uncovered terrace, so I went to the local sports shop to purchase a jacket to keep me warm and dry. I returned to the pub with said jacket, only to discover that the game had been postponed. The return trip, on the Monday of the Championship, coupled with the silly games which included 'Loud' having to crawl up and down the aisle of the train barking like a dog as a forfeit, made it all worthwhile.

Colin Carr

I decided to come back from a trip to the Czech Republic a couple of days early to get to Cardiff. Wandering along the road to Ninian Park about 2 p.m., I met John Chuku and others coming the other way. 'Game off?' I inquired, surprised. 'No, it was a 12 p.m. kick-off because of the Welsh international at Anfield this evening' came the reply. The game had been rescheduled a week or two before and I didn't know. The longest abortive trip to an Argyle game – 900 miles!

Phil Rescorla

The Wembley play-off final, the invasion of Hartlepool by the Green Army for the ultimately meaningless 8-1 mauling and the heartache of relegation at Burnley were all incredibly memorable matches. However, my most memorable trip is the 2003 pre-season tour of Austria, accompanied by fellow Greens John Lloyd, Toby Jones, Paul Luxton and Neil Carhart. How many grounds do you get to by walking along a train line? That's the route we took from the town's only bar to Pettenbach's ground where Argyle played Bundesliga B outfit Wacker Berghausen. Outside the ground, we were greeted by the 'stadium' announcer, Uber, who was an absolute star. His son had previously visited Plymouth on a student exchange and thought it was 'a very beautiful city'. The poor boy obviously hadn't seen much of the world! Probably the most surreal experience of my life is the only way to describe seeing the Greens line up in front of the main stand while the national anthems were played on the PA system. Not content with that overindulgence, the referee then asked the Wacker players to walk along the line shaking hands with the Argyle team in true international tradition. The match itself was very dull, but it didn't stop Argyle fans from singing their hearts out for most of the match, including several chants for Gordon Sparks who was reporting on the match for BBC Radio Devon, and our new best mate Uber. We enjoyed the relaxed approach to drinking in Austria, which meant that you could watch the match with pints in hand. Afterwards, most of the crowd ended up having a kick about on the pitch, while the female contingent of the North Devon Greens surrounded Jason Bent, demanding snogs! Later that week, we watched Austria Vienna play Arsenal, which was even more surreal, as there were as many Argyle fans as UK-based Gooners. Dennis Bergkamp seemed particularly bemused to hear 'Bergkamp is a Pilgrim' chants coming from the terraces. We had a great laugh with the Arsenal fans as our chant of 'You're just a small town in Barnet' was met with a chorus of 'We hate Exeter'. Then we drove on to Schwanenstadt where Argyle played in a triangular competition with lower-league Austrian side Schwanenstadt and Romanian top-flight outfit Petrolul Astra Ploiesti. Our pre-match meal was eaten in 35-degree heat with beautiful views over a lake surrounded by mountains in Gmunden. It couldn't have been more different from the pre-match pubs normally visited during the course of a season in such beauty spots as Macclesfield, Hartlepool and Stockport. While driving to Schwanenstadt, there was a distinct smell of burning in our hire car. Showing typical Janner intelligence, we stopped to check where the smell was coming from and discovered flames under one of the wheels! And where did we stop to allow the car to cool off? A bloody petrol station! Argyle ended up losing 1-0 to the excellent Romanians and drawing 0-0 with the hosts in two 45-minute matches. It was very amusing to hear the Schwanenstadt announcer encouraging the Argyle fans to stay for the last tournament between the hosts and Astra by explaining that the beer tent was staying open! The trip became even more bizarre in Salzburg after the tournament as we bumped into a gaggle of Austrian ladies out on a hen night, sang 'Eng-er-land, Eng-er-land, Eng-er-land' to Prince Charles' motorcade as he returned from the Salzburg Festival, and ended up in the same dodgy bar as the Argyle squad who were bonding over a couple of shandies. It was a fantastic experience to follow Argyle around picturesque Austria and meet many amusing characters. It was just a shame that when I returned home I had to endure my friends taking the proverbial out of me for going all that way without seeing an Argyle goal, let alone a win. Typical bleddy Argyle!

Dan King

7 Why do you support Argyle?

I blame my dad, Phil, who would blame his. His dad was stationed in Plymouth during the war and stayed afterwards. I've never lived there, but used to visit as a kid in the mid-Seventies, when the seed was sown. I heard someone describe supporting the Greens as like having a strange virus that you cannot shake off. Whilst all the kids around me at school supported Liverpool, I was the freaky one with the green-and-white scarf and an obsessive interest in Paul Mariner! The thing is, through thick and thin, I am always happy to tell people who I support, and in many cases I am remembered because of my allegiances. Take my current workplace, where my nickname is Pilgrim, in the land of Blades and Owls. Wherever I go, people remember me because of Argyle.

Chris Ramsay

I started going to games when I was five or six. My uncle would pick me up from my house on his way from the pub, and we'd go to the Lyndhurst End with his mates. I'd stand on the concrete footing of the floodlights between the Lyndhurst and the Devonport and both enjoy the game and learn all kinds of new vocabulary from the cries and yells of my uncle and his mates. My first heroes were Pat Dunne and Mike Bickle, and I still remember what I thought were the best Argyle shirts, in basically white with a green-and-black band across the middle. For years afterwards, there was something (the speakers?) at the Barn Park End painted with that design. I followed Argyle through thick and thin then, through the Furnell years, the glory of the Mariner and Rafferty days (although my favourite was Hugh McAuley), the disappointing relegations and then Third Division drudgery for years after.

Steve Lynch

My Auntie Peg was the one who planted the seed and ensured my blood ran green from then on. She was a member of the supporters' club committee, and she would take me to sell handbooks, rosettes and golliwogs in a hut at the top of the Barn Park terracing. Having been corrupted by my aunt to all things green myself, I clearly had to make sure my own children were similarly treated. My elder son's first match was at Fellowes Park against Walsall – a friendly, atmospheric ground, not at all like Bescot. His mother insisted he take a book to read in case he was bored! Argyle won and he has been a convert ever since. In fact, for the next fifteen matches, mostly away, he didn't see them lose – quite a record. My younger son's first match was the fifth round tie at The Hawthorns, when Tommy scored the winner. He told his mother he was surprised that his father had stood on his seat when Argyle scored – clearly, he had a lot to learn.

Kevin Howarth

A life sentence passed on by my dad. He was more of a football supporter than an Argyle fan. But, once I visited Home Park, I wanted more and more and more. It is now more about identity, I think, having moved away from the area in 1978. Within my own work and local circles, I'm famous for it. No one I spend time with knows any other Argyle fans! That's it then … I'm unique. That must be it. Without getting too philosophical about it, it's interesting to question what it is I do support. It's not the players themselves – they come and go of course. It's not the board or the management – they do too. It's actually the name and the shirt and Semper Fidelis.

Malcolm Sheryn

I grew up in Somerset in a family in which no one else was the least bit interested in football. I had a bedroom plastered with posters from *Shoot* magazine and spent hours kicking a soft ball around the house. It probably annoyed the hell out of my parents. It wasn't until I was 27 that I finally ended up in a place where there was a proper football team (you can't count Bangor City, can you?). When I moved to Plymouth, I always felt that I moved home. It was a completely natural

thing for me to adopt Argyle as my first and only team.

Tim O'Hare

As a family, we moved to Plymouth in 1917, when I was 2½ years old, having been born in London. I very much remember standing on the terrace and, by the time I was 12 or 13, a younger brother and I had season tickets for that area. There were steps in those days. I returned to London in 1933 and the family moved up in 1937, after my father had died.

Hyman Forman

Both my parents are Plymothians. From as early as I can remember, my dad used to disappear on Saturday afternoons to watch Argyle (we lived in Liskeard at the time). Then he took me to my first match back in 1969/70. I loved it and was completely hooked! Also, my grandmother (on my mum's side) was an avid supporter and a season-ticket holder back in the 1920s and '30s. She even travelled to away matches and was a member of the supporters' club. Sadly, I never knew her, as she died before I was born. I have never lived in Plymouth as I was born in Redruth, before moving to Liskeard. Then in the early 1970s, my dad's job took the family to Kent, where I've lived ever since. However, I still have relations in Plymouth, including an aunt who lives in Lyndhurst Close, two minutes from Home Park – very handy!

Sarah Decent

I am Plymouth born and bred, and saw my first professional footie at Home Park at 12 years of age. I will never forget big Andy Nelson firing home a rare goal in a mêlée after a corner at the Barn Park End that day. I was standing right behind the goal and thought the net was going to break! I was hooked and have followed them ever since.

Bob Farmer

I support Argyle because my father took me to my first match at the age of 7 – against Scunthorpe in 1957, I think. I also support them because I was born in Plymouth and they are the local team. I think I support Argyle more in adversity than when they are successful. I also seem to be getting more hooked as I get older. Is this an unusual phenomenon? I do not think it would be the same if they ever went into the Premiership. I support Argyle the club, not any individual manager or team. I can feel as much affinity with today's team as the team of the 1960s.

John Dymot

I support Argyle because my granddad did. He took me to my first game when I was 3 and, as I grew up, he used to take me whenever we went to see him; first when he lived in Cornwall, and then when he moved to Devon. PAFC was always my first love, even when I used to watch

Palace. A few years back, when I had to make a choice, the choice was easy. I'm Argyle 'til I die.

Sue Lawrence

Well it's my local team, growing up in Cornwall, and they were the first team I went to watch and the bug got me. In a strange way, the fact that we haven't been hugely successful and won a lot gives me a sense of pride as well. It makes the sense of pride and frustration felt on the terraces all the more genuine. Whilst I love going to Home Park, I get a real buzz out of the away games. The optimism we (the fans) take with us is brilliant when, until recently, we only won two or three games away, yet we still love it. I genuinely believe other clubs envy the numbers and the volume of our away support. Whilst I want Argyle to be successful with all my heart, I hope that as supporters we do not lose that eternal optimism.

Jon Lang

I support Argyle because they are my home team and when I feel down, I can always go and watch Argyle and that cheers me up whatever the weather. But I don't thank them for the grey hairs and there are plenty of them!

Keith Frood

8 Best moment

Wembley. I saw my team win at Wembley.

Malcolm Sheryn

The one that springs to mind is the 8-1 drubbing of Hartlepool at their pitch in Shilton's promotion-that-never-was team back in 1994. I was extremely proud to be part of Argyle's history for the best away win!

Nick Sturley

The 1962 FA Cup was memorable for the two ties Argyle played. Firstly, there was the defeat of West Ham, thoroughly deserved, with an outstanding performance from Ken (Buggsy) Maloy. This was the first time I had ever seen a First Division team play. In the next round, we drew the Spurs double-winning team from 1961. The atmosphere at Home Park was incredible, even at midday, as the ground began to fill up. We lost 5-1 – but Spurs had been at Home Park with all their stars. I handed my autograph book into the changing rooms and got the whole set of signatures. (Of course, my mother disposed of it when I left home for university!) Then Malcolm Allison arrived, and Argyle played in white with the green band. I was not sure about this at the time,

although with hindsight I think it is one of the most striking kits Argyle have had. Allison's team played well, but he made some strange team choices, which did not pay off. The one that sticks in my mind is the sight of a very overweight and unfit Noel Dwyer lumbering around in goal. I went to university in Manchester in 1968 – the year United were European Champions and City were English First Division Champions. Every week, I could watch George Best, Bobby Charlton, Nobby Stiles, Colin Bell, Franny Lee and company. I remember watching that lot in the derby game at Old Trafford, and suddenly becoming very aware that 'this is alright, but I'd rather be watching Argyle!'. The most memorable match for me has to be the semi-final. I had been to the quarter-final at Home Park and marvelled at Gordon Staniforth's shot that had hit both posts but not crossed the line. The replay was equally bizarre with the Andy Rogers goal direct from a corner. Dancing through the streets of Derby was quite an experience, as we were guided by the police to the station. I then had to get back to the ground to retrieve my car, but it was worth it! Villa Park was something else. The crowds and the sight of the huge bank of green and black on the terraces were things I had not experienced before. The match was exciting and, apart from the goal, was very much in Argyle's

Plymouth City Centre comes to a standstill as the Championship Trophy is paraded.

favour. There was a feeling of disappointment, of course, but we had come so near. I have not forgiven Bobby Charlton's remark before the match that he thought it was awful that Plymouth were in the semis. That continues to leave an unpleasant taste in my mouth. Of course, when we did get to Wembley, it was an amazing afternoon as well. The match was a rather dour one and very evenly contested. I felt amazingly confident about the outcome, which is quite unusual for me. The whole family were there, including my daughter. If you pause the official video about seven seconds after the final whistle, you can actually see us! But the singing afterwards was unlike anything I have ever heard from Argyle fans and stays in my memory. So we come to this last promotion. I think this was the best season yet. But I live in hope of even better. Come on you Greens!

Kevin Howarth

I think it has to be the 2001/02 season, culminating in the last game *v.* Cheltenham. I think the whole season had completely re-ignited the green flame that burns within me, not that it was ever entirely extinguished, but it has certainly been flickering over the previous seasons. Everything about that season was exciting, not just the Championship, but the great atmosphere the rebuilt stadium was creating, the brilliant manager, the new board and a team that was really together and playing for each other and their club. I don't think I'd ever been so optimistic ...

Sarah Decent

As a result of Argyle's history of failure and underachievement, I can well remember any contrasting moments of uncontained joy and pleasure while supporting them. They tend to be away from home, as that is where the years of suffering are most acute, and so the highs are therefore more powerful. When the fifth goal went in at the Hawthorns for a 5-2 victory on Easter Monday 1993, it was the first away hammering I had seen us give a team. I yelled and screamed and hugged people I didn't know on that sparse old terrace, like I never had before. I didn't know this could happen to Plymouth. Some of my best moments came during the cacophonous support at Brentford during our 1-1 draw. It was the most intense celebration of being an Argyle fan that I can remember. Without a doubt, the top of the shop was on the pitch at Rochdale after winning promotion in 2002. Over twenty years of home matches, and over ten years of travelling to away games as well, told, on the whole, a tale of suffering. I was there for promotion in 1986, but I had not invested as much emotional currency by that point. Wembley in 1996 was more a relief to be promoted through the back door of the play-offs. But recently, we had 'established' ourselves in the Fourth Division (call it by its proper name), and until the 2001/02 season, our away form had been a joke for years. That season, we topped the table from October and were formidable away from home. But years of letdowns had not let anyone become convinced of promotion until it was indisputable. When Lee Hodges had lifted the third high into the Rochdale net, it was real. On the pitch after the match, as I stood looking up at the players celebrating in the stand before us, a flood of Argyle memories rushed through my head, and a feeling that we, the supporters, bloody well deserved this. And that perhaps I would not see the like of such a season again, so make the best of it while I could. It was the best of times.

Toby Jones

Beating Wimbledon away in the League Cup in the David Kemp era was a good night. We knew an assault was coming from the Dons, but how would Argyle cope? Very well, was the answer! The Greens dealt with the bombardment and hit them twice on the break – a fine, professional performance against a First (old First, that is) Division side. I felt 10 feet tall walking down the street afterwards, genuinely proud to follow the club. Some of the defeats in the past have led to some pretty good moments too! The gallows humour after Argyle defeats in the bleak days of the past has meant tears of laughter, when despair seemed the only emotion possible.

John Williams

I guess my best moment supporting Argyle would have to be the end of the final game of the 2001/02 season when the Division Three Championship trophy was presented at Home Park. Because I produce match reports for the Argyle website, I was allowed down onto the pitch while the ceremony took place and was standing on the centre circle, directly in front of the players, as the trophy was handed over. I'm still looking for a photo that has me in it, though! The atmosphere was awesome.

My clearest impression from that day was actually from just before the players came out onto the pitch after the game. One of the presentation party came out with all the players' medals hanging on their arm, and I can distinctly remember the absolutely magical tinkling sound they made as they went past me. That was a pretty unique memory. The other best moment was after the Rochdale game in the same season when Argyle clinched promotion. I was at home listening to dual commentaries (Gordon Sparks on Radio Devon and, with a slight delay, Steve Hill on the Argyle website). When the final whistle blew, I was online sharing thoughts with Argyle fans worldwide and reading congratulatory messages from fans of other clubs – it was a really special illustration of the nature of the online community that follows Argyle.

Tim O'Hare

I have had a few 'best moments' supporting Argyle. The first was on Tuesday 15 April 1975, when Argyle clinched promotion by beating Colchester 1-0 at Home Park. As I – along with thousands of others – was going over the fence at the Devonport End at the end of the game, it collapsed. Luckily, no one was seriously hurt. It was strange clinching the promotion at home as it was won on the back of some tremendous away performances – in what was my first season of following the Greens away. (Charlton 2-0, Bournemouth 7-3, Watford 3-1, Hereford 5-1, Tranmere 3-1) The run-in to the 1985/86 promotion was tremendous – and was capped with the 4-0 drubbing of 'local rivals' Bristol City at Home Park. The game had been postponed at Easter because the pitch was waterlogged and, on the night, there must have been around 30,000 in the ground, although the official attendance was 19,600. Season 2000/01 did not have much going for it as far as Argyle was concerned, but it was the season that Argyle fans at last became active. Having had several years of negativity towards McCauley, this was the season of 'positivity' with the aborted NYD@LOFC, BIG@BARNET and BIGGER@HOME PARK culminating in the wonderful evening at the Cooperage with the fantastic Jellyroll Jackson & The Boogie Kings. These events made me prouder than ever to be an Argyle fan. Finally, I can't fail to mention 2001/02 – a fantastic season all around, but in particular clinching promotion at away matches, where only the true fans are in attendance, with no hangers-on. Rochdale was excellent and Darlington was even better as following the celebrations in the ground, the party continued in the supermarket car park. I think we eventually drove out of the town about 10.30 p.m. with 'Tubthumping' on the car stereo. Never has a song seemed more apt – 'I get knocked down, but I get up again, you're never gonna keep me down … '

Steve Nicholson

The players celebrate on the podium, as assistant coach and former player Kevin Summerfield looks on.

Without any doubt whatsoever, the game at Darlington in the 2001/02 season was one of the best moments in the whole time that I have supported our team. They were absolutely magnificent. The happiest time was at Rochdale, just a few games earlier, but the Wembley visit in 1996, whilst memorable, was unbearable for me and I did not enjoy it because of the terrible tension that I felt throughout.

Ken Jones

Having once opted to visit a sick relative rather than watch the Aston Villa versus Argyle game shows my intense dislike of the game of football. But to now say that an Argyle double-header weekend is one of my most memorable experiences ever shows the effect football can have on your life. The whole weekend in Carlisle/ Darlington was exhausting, exhilarating, exciting, but most of all, unexplainable!! The feeling of running onto the pitch at the Darlington game, with Lisa Sturrock by my side, and both of us just jumping onto our respective dads is a feeling that nearly brought us both to tears! We had watched the game with all the supporters, and under the watchful eye of my brother, Ollie, and his friend, Terry (director Phill Gill's son). We sat down when they sang 'Stand up if you love Darlington'; we hugged random strangers when we scored, and from about the seventieth minute onwards, all of us prepared ourselves for the most memorable run of our lives – onto the pitch. First on was my brother, closely followed by more supporters. Lisa and I ran our fastest –

and you could even see us on the high-lights of that game on the television. We managed to clamber into the tunnel, amid the clamour of supporters, stewards and officials. After scrambling to the directors' box, surrounded by all the team, we managed to look out at what Argyle had achieved. A crowd of around 800 Argyle fans were chanting every song that had ever been sung on the terraces of Home Park. Championship champagne was handed around, and it seemed that every-one was sipping from the bottle of success. Fifteen minutes later, we came back down to the players' dressing room, where we were politely told to wait outside the door as it wasn't appropriate for us to be in a room of twenty-one barely dressed, highly ecstatic men. Me, being sixteen, and Lisa three years my senior, didn't exactly agree – but did as we were told. Fortunately, the dressing-room door was wedged open, and every so often a bottle of Championship champagne was passed around. The coach journey home was an amazing way to top off what had been a fantastic weekend. Crate after crate of beer, alcopops and champagne were being loaded onto the coach. It was deemed 'Karaoke Night' on the way home, and five toilet stops and twenty-five songs later, we arrived back at Home Park. It was 7.15 a.m., and I had just one hour and forty-five minutes to get myself ready for school that day. However, even though I had had no sleep in forty-eight hours, nothing could remove the per-manent grin I had on my face that day. Thank you, Argyle.

Lucy Stapleton

9 The FA Cup run

The first round – the omens weren't good. Argyle were drawn away to Southend United and they hadn't won at Roots Hall since a 1-0 Third Division (South) victory in 1956/57. So, most of us expected that Argyle would fall at the first hurdle yet again and that we would have a free Saturday to go Christmas shopping in December. I don't remember much about the match to be honest, apart from the fact that it was freezing cold. I was stood on the open terracing at Roots Hall with a mate from Torpoint. We'd enjoyed a few cans of breakfast on the train and had continued to take on fuel when we reached London. By the time we got to Southend, we were both pretty polluted and as the more pleasant effects of the alcohol wore off, the somewhat less welcome ones kicked in. And so it was that we stood shivering on a windblown terrace in darkest Essex watching two very poor football teams trying to win a place in the second round of the FA Cup. The game finished 0-0. Given Argyle's aforementioned record against the Shrimpers, we should maybe have realised that this was to be no ordinary season for the Greens, but we could never have known what was to come. The replay took place the following Wednesday at Home Park and, after 90 minutes of unremitting grimness, the two sides had still failed to muster a goal

between them. It was highly appropriate that the first goal of the tie was an own goal, Southend's Mickey Stead turning the goal past his own 'keeper in the first half of extra time. Tommy Tynan later made the tie safe.

The second round – Argyle's hard-earned but less-than-glorious victory in the first round was rewarded by a pairing with another club from the land of the white stiletto, as Southern League Barking made the trip down to Home Park. Argyle were struggling in the Third Division and there was a very real fear that Home Park would be staging Fourth Division football for the first time the following season. So it wasn't surprising that the non-Leaguers fancied their chances, and they certainly gave Argyle a good run for their money. A rare goal from Mark Rowe and another from Lyndsey Smith saw Argyle to a decidedly shaky 2-1 victory. It would be fair to say that Cup fever had not yet gripped the city, as a mere 4,754 hardy souls turned out to watch this match – almost 800 less than had witnessed the first-round replay against Southend.

The third round – in the far and distant times before Teletext, the internet, digital television and text messaging, the draw for the third round of the FA Cup was one of

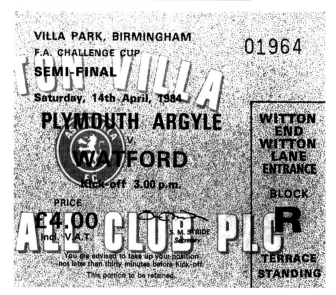

FA Cup semi-final ticket.

the most exciting days in the football calendar. The big guns of the First Division came into the frame where they could be matched with anyone. There were always a few non-League teams who'd survived three rounds already, and the Cup would throw up, as it still does, some tantalising ties. It wasn't done much differently than it is today, except that it was done by a couple of faceless officials from the FA and broadcast live on Monday lunchtime on Radio Two. Despite the lack of glitz, see-through rotating drums (they still used the velvet bags then) and Z-list celebrities, I believe it was actually much more enjoyable. You weren't informed of any of the numbers of the more fancied teams (although they were easy enough to work out as numbers 1 to 44 were the teams in the First and Second Divisions in alphabetical order), so there was a certain dramatic quality to it. There was also a good long pause after the number was read out. 'Number 53 ... Plymouth Argyle' (great, we're at home, who we gonna get?

Liverpool? Man Utd?) 'Will play number 49 ... (sod it, it's a small team. Still, at least we've got a chance of getting to the fourth round) ... Newport County (oh great)'. Newport, like Southend, were in the same division as us and were quite a few places higher in the table. Barely a fortnight before we met them in the Cup, I went to Somerton Park where we lost 2-0, thanks to two goals by future Liverpool and Republic of Ireland striker John Aldridge. After the game, I was in the players' bar, courtesy of an old Torpoint school friend who played for Newport at the time, Roy Carter. Argyle's new striker, who'd yet to really settle in at Home Park, was one Tommy Tynan, who had been signed the previous summer from the Welsh club. He was dropped for the League match against Newport and the word on the terraces was that he was going back to reform his partnership with Aldridge. He certainly seemed a lot more comfortable in the company of the Newport players after the match than he did with his new teammates. Aldridge repeated his Somerton Park trick at Home Park with another brace of goals, the second of these coming about as a result of a dreadful mix-up in the Argyle defence as late as the 84th minute. It seemed that Argyle were going to be able to concentrate on avoiding relegation to the Fourth Division when, in injury time, a foul by Roy Carter (good lad!) gave the Greens a lifeline they barely deserved – penalty! Amidst the euphoria surrounding this late chance of a reprieve, there were some dark mutterings amongst the Lyndhurst faithful when none other than Tommy Tynan stepped up to take the spot-kick against his old mates. Believe it or not, this future Argyle legend had not exactly endeared himself to the Green Army during the early days of his Home Park career. He had come to the club with a rep-utation as a goalscorer, and had so far man-aged only 5 goals in 20-odd appearances. He also appeared to have a bit of an atti-tude problem and seemed a pale imitation of previous goalscoring heroes like Paul Mariner, David Kemp or Fred Binney. Many there that day fully expected him to miss the penalty and to return to Newport County in the not-too-distant future, but cometh the hour, cometh the man, and Tommy calmly converted the penalty in the way which was to become familiar to us all in later years and Argyle had a replay. There's a bloke in Torpoint (who shall remain nameless) who I will never forgive for this. The replay at Newport was the only game I missed during our historic cup run and it was all down to him. Neither I, nor my mate, who'd accompanied me to Southend, drove at this time, but we had arranged a lift to Newport for the replay. We were all geared up to go when we both had phone calls on the afternoon of the match from our 'mate' who informed us that he wasn't going, as 'something had come up'. It was too late to arrange alter-native transport, so we resigned ourselves to listening out for the infrequent and sketchy reports on Radio Devon. This, of course, we decided to do in a pub, which proved not to be a great idea as the land-lord, despite our constant pleading, would-n't switch the radio on. To be honest, we, like most Argyle fans, were fairly pes-simistic about our chances in the replay. After all, we'd only just lost there in the League and our form since that defeat had certainly not got any better. The apathy sur-rounding this Cup replay was almost deaf-ening. No one in the pub was remotely interested and, due to the landlord's afore-mentioned intransigence, there was no way we could find out the score. I even phoned Home Park, but there was no answer, so, having obtained the number from Directory Enquiries, I put in a call to Newport County. A woman answered the phone and I asked her the score. '1-0', she said. 'Oh', I replied. 'To Plymouth', she added. I can only hope she's got her hear-ing back by now. The annoying postscript to this chapter of the Cup run is that the next day I found out that my 'mate' had decided to go to Newport after all, but had neglected to tell us. I've just about got over it now, but it was bloody annoying at the time, with the only saving grace being that the idiot managed to take the wrong turn-ing at the M4/M5 intersection and was halfway to Birmingham when he ran out of petrol. He eventually got home at about seven o'clock the following morning – served him right.

The fourth round – Unlike the previous round, there was no need to sit huddled around a radio to discover who our next opponents would be. Due to the third-round game requiring a replay, we'd already been through that; in fact, I'd not even bothered listening as I was sure we would lose at Newport. The back page of Monday's *Herald* stated that, should we be successful in the replay, we'd be playing at home in the fourth round against Darlington. This was hardly the glamour tie we wanted. This was Argyle's first foray as far as the fourth round since the glorious 1974/75 season, when a capacity 38,000 crowd had seen us lose to Everton at Home Park. Still, at least there was a live chance of progress as Darlington were a Fourth Division side, and the prospect of only a second-ever appearance in the last sixteen of the competition, where you were almost guaranteed a 'glamour' draw, was a very real one. Still, the fever was yet to grip the city as less than 9,000 turned out to watch Argyle struggle to overcome the Quakers in the first ever meeting between the two clubs. It's strange how many memorable encounters there have been between the two teams when you bear in mind we'd never played them before 1984. Darlo, in front of a sizeable and noisy band of supporters who'd made the long trek down from the north-east, managed to get their noses in front, and an equaliser was not looking likely until local boy John 'Bonehead' Uzzell thundered home a header just before half-time. The second half saw Darlington looking more likely to snatch the victory than Argyle until, in the 81st minute, Tommy Tynan's strike partner Gordon Staniforth fired home a shot from the edge of the box to give Argyle a 2-1 victory. It was to be Stani's only goal of the Cup campaign, but he was to play

more than a bit part in the drama that was to come.

Neil Jenkins

The fifth round – I don't think I'll ever forget the West Brom game. On the way up, we stopped at the West Bromwich Moat House for a few bevvies. We didn't realise that it was also the HQ for the West Brom squad. My dad, who was already quite pissed, spotted Giles, the Baggies manager, and pushed his way through the mêlée to talk to him. I sat with a group of mates, cringing with embarrassment until my dad came back. 'Oh no, what did you say to him?' I asked. 'Oh, I was quite polite,' said my dad. 'I said, "You're gonna get a right arsin'."' At the ground, we all cheered when Noddy appeared, and then made an even bigger noise for Umbrella Vi. Nothing was going to stop us that day. Afterwards, we all cheered in the car when Argyle got mentioned on *Sports Report*. On the M5, the hard shoulders were full of dancing, urinating Janners. Our carload stopped at a pub in Worcester. I had to drink Kaliber because I was driving. Father lined up another three or four Gold Labels.

Efford Boy

The fifth round – Argyle had huffed, puffed, struggled and ridden their luck to get this far and had not been rewarded with a mouth-watering tie that would bring much needed revenue into the club. In addition, the Cup run was causing a backlog of League fixtures to build up, which was bound to cause problems towards the end of the season, given

Argyle's perilous position in the Third Division. And so it was, that the following Monday, we all gathered around our radios again, hoping for that plum draw which would give Argyle a good injection of cash and the chance of a glorious exit. For only the second time in the run, we were drawn away from home – at West Brom. The Baggies were a reasonable First Division side at that time (although they were soon to fall from grace), who, in recent years, had even had a decent crack at the title and had had regular experience of European competition. It wasn't the best draw we could have had, West Brom weren't exactly glamorous, but there was a chance we could go up there and avoid a hammering. We'd take a decent number of supporters and, although Argyle weren't exactly a big draw, West Brom would have a good crowd, so the takings, of which Argyle would have a share, would be quite healthy. It was the best we could hope for really – an honourable defeat and a few bob in the bank. I worked with a West Brom fan at the time, a lad called Bonzo Jones, who's still a good mate to this day. So confident was he that the Baggies would give Argyle a good stuffing, that he decided not to go to the match, but he was taking bets all round town that West Brom would win – he'd even give us the draw. They were only small bets – a quid here, a fiver there (I had a fiver's worth) – but there were a lot of them, and he was expecting a decent little windfall. The previous season had seen Argyle reach the third round of the Cup when we were drawn away to Watford, who were flying high in the First Division at the time. I'd decided to run a coach trip to this match from Torpoint, and we'd ended up having a brilliant day out, despite Argyle losing 2-0 in

quite gallant fashion. In fact, if Kevin Hodges had had his shooting boots on and a bit more luck at Vicarage Road that day, it would have been a different story (and they say lightning never strikes twice). After the match, we'd all headed into the West End and had a great night out before arriving home, hungover and bleary-eyed, on Sunday morning. A few of the lads who'd been on that trip asked me if I'd organise a similar excursion to the West Brom game, so I made a few calls, organised a coach, arranged a pub near Bristol to stop in on the way back and managed to almost fill the coach within a couple of days. So, on the morning of the match, we all met at the Torpoint Ferry, crossed the river and boarded the coach. There were a couple of spare seats, and one of these was taken by a mate of mine called Oggie, who just happened to be on the Devonport side of the river on his way home from nightshift when we got off the ferry. He hadn't intended to go, but he had little choice in the matter really as about half-a-dozen of the lads grabbed him and bundled him onto the coach, holding him down until we were the other side of Ivybridge, by which time he'd become resigned to his fate. The beer was flowing and there was a faint whiff of some exotic-smelling smoke emanating from certain sections of the coach. The atmosphere was great, there was no expectancy – just the prospect of a good day out, a few beers, and the ambition to make more noise than the West Brom fans, whatever was happening on the pitch. By the time we'd passed Bristol, the atmosphere had changed a little. The beer was running out and, as we were making good time, some of the lads were suggesting that it may be a good idea to stop at a pub. I had a word with the driver and he was quite happy to do this, as long as we only stopped for an hour. We got off the motorway and found a pub. I did the decent thing and went and asked the landlord if he could entertain a coachload of Argyle fans for an hour. Bearing in mind that this was the mid-Eighties and football violence was pretty widespread, it came as no surprise that he wasn't having any of it, so I got back on the coach and explained the situation to a chorus of boos and catcalls. The next pub we stopped at elicited the same response, and by now some of the lads (and, it must be said, lasses – of whom a couple had expressed a desire to join the 'M5 Club', an earthbound version of the 'Mile-High Club') were getting downright mutinous. There was only one thing for it. The next pub we saw would not be consulted in the matter – we would simply get off the coach and pour in. And so it was that The Cross Keys at Hardwick, Gloucestershire became a favoured haunt of travelling Argyle fans from Torpoint. There were two old – and I mean old – girls behind the bar, and they were not really prepared for 50-odd thirsty travellers. This quickly became evident when they spent about ten minutes trying to serve the first customer, and it was at that point that some of our gallant band decided to take matters into their own hands. In our contingent, there were at least half-a-dozen people who either ran or worked in pubs. One of these volunteered to change a barrel for the two old ladies when the lager went, and a couple more people offered their services as temporary barstaff. The two old girls, who were completely non-plussed, decided to take up these offers, and so it was that Oggie (who, you may remember, had just come off nightshift and who should have been at home with his missus, who still didn't know his whereabouts) ended up behind the bar. I was his first customer and my round of three pints and a large brandy was quickly totted up in his head. 'Four pence', he said, 'It's happy hour – penny a drink'. Fair enough, I thought. At these prices, it would have been rude not to drink as much as was humanly possible in the short time we had in this fine establishment, so we all did our best. We also availed ourselves freely of the fine food that someone had thoughtfully left in the kitchen – pork pies, sandwiches etc., possibly prepared for some function later in the day. Thankfully, by the time we left, my brother and I had decided that this was taking things a little far and organised a whip-round for the two old girls. Everybody was very public-spirited about this and most of them bunged in probably more than they would have spent had they been paying the correct prices. We presented the cash to the ladies before we left and they both smiled sweetly and wished us bon voyage. And so, to the match. I guess you all know what happened, but here it is anyway. Before the match, West Brom had introduced their new management team of Johnny Giles, Norman Hunter and Nobby Stiles, who were greeted with thunderous applause by the expectant home support. The new 'dream team' and the supporters then settled down to watch their team dispose of little Argyle with ease. It was not to be. Argyle quickly settled and were playing with purpose, determination and no little skill – they were unrecognisable from the team struggling in the Third Division. They were passing the ball around comfortably and West Brom were, at times, chasing shadows. The sense of unease around the home sections of the ground was palpable. When the half-time whistle went, most of us in the Argyle end were cursing Argyle's inability to score whilst on top – we had dominated the first half, but it was still 0-0 and we couldn't possibly play like that again in the second half. We didn't. We were better, and the West Brom players were getting shakier by the minute. Just before the hour mark, Gordon Staniforth chased a ball that didn't deserve chasing out to the left-hand side of West Brom's penalty area, caught it, looked up and laid the ball perfectly into the path of Tommy Tynan, who cracked the ball past former Argyle 'keeper Paul Barron into the West Brom net. The Argyle end of the stadium, which had already been very noisy, erupted, and all of a sudden we sobered up and girded ourselves for what we expected to be a long half-hour. This had now ceased to be a 'nice day out' – this was serious, history-in-the-making stuff. We were beating a First Division side away from home in the FA Cup – no Argyle side had done that before – and we were half-an-hour away from the quarter-final – another first. The expected West Brom onslaught never happened. Save for a late header over the bar by Garry Thompson, the Baggies offered nothing. If anything, it was Argyle who looked more likely to score and when the final whistle went, the West Midlands experienced its second sonic boom of the day. There were grown men crying tears of joy and everywhere you looked there were people hugging like long-lost brothers. We'd just witnessed what was, in my opinion, one of the finest performances by an Argyle team ever – it had been a magical afternoon. The planned pub stop on the way home didn't happen. Apparently, there'd been

some minor altercations involving Argyle supporters, although, it must be said, the majority behaved impeccably, as did the West Brom fans we met outside the ground, who all offered their congratulations and best wishes for the next round. There were police cars at every motorway junction on the M5, so we decided to forego the arranged stop at The Anchor at Filton and head for home. A clear road and an eager driver ensured that we were back in Torpoint for 9 o'clock, which gave us plenty of time for the traditional Torpoint run of twice round the six pubs of Fore Street and then down the Harbour Lights. Oggie's missus was surprised to see him, as were some of the other wives and girlfriends who'd taken advantage of their partners' absence by going out by themselves (or not, in a couple of cases) on a Saturday night for a change. I was actually unattached at this time, but this situation was rectified – on a strictly one-night-only basis – at the Harbour Lights later that evening, although I must admit she was slightly confused by the shout of 'Tynan … YEEEEEEEEESSSSSS' at a certain critical moment in our brief relationship. They just don't get it, do they? The finest moment (well, second finest, then) was when we – all fifty of us – walked into the Jubilee and saw a crestfallen-looking Bonzo Jones sitting on his own at the end of the bar with a pile of fivers and pound notes in front of him.

The quarter-final – there were now eight teams left in the FA Cup: Argyle, six from the First Division, and a lone representative of the Second Division, Derby County, who were struggling in the League and very close to going out of business. From wanting to be drawn against a big club in the last round, the general consensus of opinion now was that we were only two matches from Wembley, so we wanted the easiest draw we could get. It wouldn't have mattered if we'd drawn Manchester United or Modbury – this was the quarter-final of the FA Cup and whoever we played and wherever we played, it would be a sellout, so the money was not an issue any more. We wanted the draw that offered the best chance to progress to the semi-final, which would be Derby at home, and that was exactly what we got. Derby's financial state at this time was so bad that there was even talk that they may well fold before the match could take place. Although this would mean a huge loss of revenue for Argyle in terms of gate receipts and all the other benefits of having 35,000 people turn up for a football match, there were many who were secretly praying it would happen. I'm glad to say I wasn't one of them, and I'm also glad it didn't happen. By now, the apathy surrounding Argyle's Cup run had disappeared. You couldn't open a paper or switch on a local radio station without someone voicing an opinion. People who hadn't set foot in Home Park for years or, in some cases, ever, were all offering their suggestions for which formation we should play or who should be dropped. A long-time supporter of the club, Umbrella Vi, became something of a local celebrity. She was a regular caller to Louise Churchill's phone-in programme on Plymouth Sound and, during the latter stages of the Cup run, she was invariably the first caller of the day, talking of nothing but her beloved Argyle. To be honest, it seemed like there was nothing else to talk about for those few weeks. The game against Derby at Home Park was probably

the biggest ever in Argyle's history at that point. You could argue (and I would agree) that games where promotion is achieved are more important in the long term. In terms of attendance, there had been bigger games – a few 40,000-plus gates in the distant past and, in more recent times, the 38,000 crowds for the matches against Everton in '75 and the friendly against Santos in '73. But this was the quarter-final of the FA Cup with all the magic that conjures up. There are a few clubs who could possibly be a little blasé about an FA Cup quarter-final – Manchester United, Arsenal and Liverpool perhaps – but even some of the supposedly big clubs like Spurs, Chelsea or Leeds would still feel that this was a big occasion. If you aren't old enough to have experienced that day, then think of Wembley in '96 or the Cheltenham home match in April 2002 and you're getting close. They were equally nerve-tingling and emotional and, as I mentioned, definitely more important, but there's something about the FA Cup. The build-up to the match was incredible. It was difficult to get any work done, the city centre shops were decked in green, black and white. Everybody wanted to talk about Argyle. There were some dissenting voices – 'Bleddy 'ell, it's only a bleddy game o' furtball – what's all the bleddy fuss about?' – but they were few and far between. For many, it was going to be a day to be enjoyed and savoured, no matter what happened, but for the diehards, it was going to be agony. If we'd been knocked out in the first, second or even third round, it would have been forgotten about by now and we'd all be concentrating on the struggle against relegation. If we'd lost to Darlington in the fourth round, we'd probably still be having pangs of disappointment – we'd all have been certain we'd have drawn Liverpool at home in the fifth if we'd got through. If we'd lost at West Brom, we'd have thought fair enough – we had a good run, made a few quid and lost to a First Division club – no disgrace in that. But we were past that stage now, we were two matches from Wembley, we could even win the bloody thing – we only need a couple of fluky goals. To the faithful, there were to be no more 'nice days out' – we wanted to win. And so the day dawned. A typical March day, a bit windy, coldish, grey in the way that only Plymouth can be grey – a non-descript sort of day really, hardly befitting such an occasion. I went to the game with my brother – I wanted to be with a fellow 'real' Argyle fan and to keep away from the hangers-on as I felt I couldn't be responsible for my actions if we lost. I'd be gutted and I'd have difficulty understanding why they weren't feeling as bad as I did. To them, it would be the end of an adventure, whereas to me it would feel like the end of the world. The main decisions were things like where to get a pint. The pubs in Stoke [Damerel] were going to be packed, so that was pointless, plus there'd probably be a fair bit of trouble, so we decided to start early in Torpoint then get the ferry at about one and walk up to the ground. The Wheelers was packed within five minutes of opening, there was green, black and white as far as the eye could see and the atmosphere was fantastic. There were even a couple of Derby fans in there, matelots from *HMS Raleigh*, but they were welcomed although they had to take a bit of good-natured stick. We drank a couple and then crossed the river and began the long walk up to Home Park. Stoke was busy, as expected, but there was

a mate of a mate working as doorman at the Stoke Social Club who spotted us and let us in. It was quiet compared with the pubs, although everyone in there was going to the match, so we stayed for a couple and then walked up to the ground. For the first time in years, Home Park and its environs felt like a real football ground. There were hot-dog stands, blokes selling dodgy merchandise, police horses and a real buzz about the place for the first time since the promotion season in 1974/75. There were a few skirmishes between rival groups of supporters in the car park, but nothing serious – far less than expected really, given the times we were living in. We got into the ground and, incredibly, managed to get fairly close to our usual spot in the Lyndhurst, or Popular Side, as we'd always called it. Even more remark-ably, some of our usual fellow fans had also managed to get to their usual spots – a crowd of lads who came up from Falmouth for every home game. We didn't know their names and never met them outside the confines of Home Park, but we'd chat to them at every home match and, over the years, had become mates in a strange, Argyle sort of way. It was good to see them amongst the crowd of unfa-miliar faces. There was a marching band on the pitch before the game. This was a strange sight at a football ground by the mid-Eighties and it harked back to a bygone era of flat caps and mufflers, but it somehow seemed totally in keeping with the day and, to me, added to that special FA Cup atmosphere. The teams emerged from the tunnel (to 'Semper Fidelis' of course) and, by now, the atmosphere inside the ground was pretty intense. The Derby fans had, unusually, been put in the now-uncovered Devonport End. This somehow seemed to make them appear closer to the action than would normally be the case if they'd been put in the Barn Park End and actually enhanced the atmosphere. The 90 minutes passed so quickly. Argyle were undoubtedly the better of the two sides, but goalscoring opportunities were few and far between. The nearest Argyle came to scoring was a remarkable incident in the second half. Argyle were attacking the Devonport End when the ball broke to Gordon Staniforth about 25 yards out. He hit a ferocious drive, which hit the right-hand upright of Steve Cherry's goal. The ball then cannoned across the goalmouth, before hitting the other post and bouncing to safety. Ninety-nine times out of a hundred, the ball would have crossed the line and ended up in the net, but this was the exception to the rule. We knew then that it wasn't to be Argyle's day. Derby offered little in return and the only moment of danger was when, out of desperation, they brought on former England centre half Dave Watson to play up front for the last few minutes. He caused Argyle a few problems and nearly nicked an undeserved winner for the Rams, but the game ended up goal-less. The walk home was a miserable one. We'd had our chance and we'd blown it. There was no way we would win the replay. By the time we reached the Wheelers for a consolatory pint, Staniforth's shot was the main topic of conversation. It was offered as evidence of Derby's luck and the old 'the Cup's got their name on it' cliché was trotted out by more than a few people. A couple of people asked if I'd be running a trip to the replay the following Wednesday, but I declined. For one thing, there wasn't time to organise it and for another it would be

difficult to cover the cost, as there would be no way of filling a coach for a midweek 500-mile round trip. Of course, that didn't mean I wasn't going though. We ended up staying in the pub until closing time, re-running the match in our heads and our conversations over and over again until *Match of the Day* came on. We then all went through the agony again, and by the time the Beeb had shown Stani's shot (and, more importantly perhaps, Steve Cherry's fingertip save, of which we'd been unaware until then) for about the sixth time, we'd all convinced ourselves it had actually crossed the line. Some of the more recent converts to the green cause were even convinced that the FA would award the game to Argyle having seen this.

Neil Jenkins

The quarter-final – I remember my family made a special Argyle FA Cup hat. It was a boater, with a green Subbuteo pitch and little Subbuteo Argyle players and a goal. It was made for the Derby home quarter-final game. It was fantastic, but somebody in the crowd stole it! We never saw it again.

Sam Fleet

The quarter-final replay – I started seeing less Argyle games when I went to uni. in Bath, but my first year there coincided with the great FA Cup run. I managed to see the game in every round that year, except a replay at Newport, I think, but the one that stands out was the replay at Derby after the 0-0 tie at Home Park. There was no means from British Rail of getting back to Bath, so being a poverty-stricken student, I searched for the cheapest B&B accommodation I could get and ended up in the room of a son who was himself away at college. This room was covered in Derby County paraphernalia – scarves, posters, pennants – and when I told the owner why I was there, I got this look of pity and a 10-minute monologue of why County were going to murder us. I had the cold of all colds and was drugged up to the hilt and would have slept for days, were it not for the big game. So when I set off for the match, my legs were so heavy, I felt like resting every 5 minutes as I walked to the ground. Of course we won, and I stood behind the goal where Andy Rogers scored directly from a corner, and the walk home seemed much easier. At breakfast the next day, my cold was so bad and my voice hoarse from yelling and singing that I couldn't speak, and all I got from the owner was stony silence. To cap it off, I was able to croak a few words of delight with Harley Lawer, who was at the train station heading back to Plymouth as I was off to Bristol, and it was obvious that he was as completely joyful and excited about the whole Cup run as anybody.

Steve Lynch

The quarter-final replay – well, Wednesday couldn't come quick enough for me. Convinced we were on our way out of the Cup, I wanted to get it over and done with. I hastily arranged a day off work and contacted some lads from Kingsand who were driving up to Derby – Jim Farley and the Blagdon brothers, Pete and the late Dickie. We were on the road at about eleven and had stopped by about half-past for a couple of pints. The mood was fairly downbeat. We all believed that we'd had our chance at Home Park and that it was all over. To this day, I don't know why, but when we were coming out of a service station somewhere not too far south of Derby, I suddenly cheered up and had this strange feeling that we were going to win. More than a feeling actually, it was a bit like I've always imagined one of these moments of religious enlightenment must feel like; I didn't just think we were going to win – I KNEW we were going to win, and I knew it was going to be 1-0. I got into the car and I was smiling from ear to ear. I think the lads thought I'd had a little something to get me through the day, but I explained to them that I'd just had this overwhelming sensation that we were going to win and, suddenly, they cheered up as well. By the time we reached Derby, the car must have been positively radiating optimism. I was right behind the goal when Andy Rogers' corner swung in and over the upstretched hand of Steve Cherry. When I see the goal and the celebrations on video, I can see myself in my lucky flat cap. As soon as it went in, I knew we were home and dry. There were those around me who said we'd scored too early, but I knew that 1-0 was going to be the final score – the only time it looked in doubt was when Lyndsey Smith hit the bar and nearly upset my feeling of inner calm by making it 2-0. I can still see Chris Harrison climbing that fence in front of the fans at the end, and I can still feel the terror that I felt when, having decided to get out of Derby, we called in for a celebratory pint in Burton-on-Trent on the way home, only to find ourselves surrounded by mean, angry-looking Derby fans. Imagine my surprise and delight when they all congratulated us and wouldn't let us put our hands in our pockets. Christ knows what time we left, but I'm grateful to Jim for being so patient and putting up with three very happy drunks and not touching a drop himself.

The semi-final – the other clubs left in the competition were Everton, Southampton and Watford, and the most popular choice of opponent would be Watford. Once again, we got the draw we wanted. Villa Park was the venue nominated by the FA – pretty much the most sensible choice really, as it was easily accessible for both sets of supporters, and was certainly the most convenient big ground for Argyle fans. As soon as the draw was made, I started receiving the usual enquiries about a coach trip, so I phoned the company who'd provided the coach for the West Brom trip. Fair play to them as they said they'd had other enquiries, but were waiting for me to call them. If they hadn't, I don't think I could have organised anything, as every coach, minibus, hire car and horse-and-cart from Lands End to Taunton seemed to have been booked for this particular Saturday. The glorious day arrived and once again 'Jellytours' headed up the A38 and the M5. This time, we'd left earlier as we knew the traffic was going to be a bit heavier than it had been for West Brom and there were going to be a few more people queuing to get into the ground. A stop had been arranged at The Cross Keys again, which I'd visited between the two matches. I'd been a bit worried about going back there after our previous visit, so I'd popped in on the way to Birmingham for a non-football-related trip a week in advance. The landlord reckoned it had been the best lunch-time they'd had in the place for years and said

we'd be welcome to come back – he'd even lay on a buffet. I don't remember too much about getting to Birmingham or to Villa Park, or about the match itself really. This is not because I drank too much, it's just that the day itself was such a blur. I can remember the colours, George Reilly's goal, the one they had disallowed about 5 minutes later (thankfully – I think it could have been a hammering if that one had stood), and, of course, the Kevin Hodges shot at the end. I remember the final whistle and feeling embarrassed because I was crying, then not feeling too bad about it as I looked around and saw that most of the grown men standing near me were crying as well. I remember the team coming over to the supporters while we sang 'We're proud of you' and crying again. The trip home was the worst bit. The coach was a mixture of real Argyle fans, some floaters who'd go as long as the team were doing reasonably well, and the inevitable one-day wonders who had never even been to Home Park and had no intention of going there in the future. Once the emotions had calmed down a bit, I could actually identify the different types. The real fans were generally sitting very quietly, looking a bit melancholy, while the rest were playing cards, drinking and saying things like 'Well – it was a nice day out'. This theme continued in the local paper and on Plymouth Sound the next day. I remember a tearful Umbrella Vi phoning in, but there were too many bandwaggoners phoning in and being quoted in the paper repeating the old 'It was a nice day out' mantra. To me, it is all part of the Plymouth disease, along with apathy, cynicism and moaning – a strange mixture really. To many Argyle fans of my generation (and a few other generations), this was the greatest year in Argyle's history. I have to admit that it was exciting, although personally I preferred the promotion seasons under Tony Waiters, Dave Smith and, of course, Paul Sturrock. The trip to Wembley was better as well – because we won. I didn't have a 'nice day out' at Villa Park, I went to watch Argyle win and we lost. My dream is that Argyle become the sort of club who get regular home attendances of 20-30,000 and a travelling Green Army who, unless the team wins, don't have a 'nice day out'. I think that the absence of the latter will go a long way to making the former a reality.

PS the final – apparently Everton turned up, Watford didn't, Elton cried – I couldn't bring myself to watch it.

Neil Jenkins

The semi-final – it was a tense encounter, and I thought Argyle were unlucky not to get something out of it. In the last 10 minutes, we had Watford really rattled, but just could not find the net. A familiar story. Another element of that match was that, in streaming away from Villa Park in our thousands with my daughter and a friend of mine, we met the young man who was later to become my son-in-law. Small world.

Norman Adams

I saw both Derby games, the WBA one and the Watford match. I can't claim to have seen the whole run. The first Derby game at Home Park was probably best remembered for the Cherry save from Staniforth. The replay at the Baseball for me has two memories. One is the goal; the other is how all the Argyle fans were penned in as tight as I can remember I've ever been penned in. The other two games I watched from private hospitality or corporate boxes, which my company had at that time in the Midlands. The WBA game brings recollections not only of Tynan's goal, but also of Johnny Giles being greeted by the fans before the game as if he was the Messiah. I was as near to going through a plate-glass window at the Hawthorns when Tommy scored as anyone ever has been. I just took off! The Watford game was simply the biggest game Argyle had ever had. I saw Jim Rosenthal doing a bit for the TV outside when I arrived, and the scene was set. This was very different from anything I had ever experienced watching Argyle, before or since. The buzz, the crowds, you could even smell the anticipation of that afternoon. The game – well, we were expected to lose. We didn't let ourselves down. I never really felt gut-wrenchingly disappointed, funnily enough. It was a great day, the Watford fans contributed to that. We had a lot of banter with those who were sat outside our box, and I drove down the M1 that evening surrounded by them. Not a single bit of bad-mouthing all day. (The final, Watford v. Everton, I think was one of the poorest of all time. If only ...)

Malcolm Sheryn

I did go to the quarter-final home game against Derby and the Villa Park semi-final, but one of my high moments was at the boarding school for deaf boys in Surrey where I attended. I was in my fifth and final year and the lone Argyle fan there, as two of my Argyle mates had left a year previously. We (the boys at the school) had a blacklist of most hated football teams, which Spurs topped and, unfortunately for me, Argyle was on the list as well. I didn't know why, and still don't, but I reckon it's to do with the 'bogey' green colour. Any team Argyle played against, they supported them! Fortunately for me, the head boy, who was a mate in my form, shared the same principle as me that we should support the 'underdogs' in their success. He was behind me (well, in front of me, actually) in supporting Argyle in the FA Cup run and he threatened any boy who tried to intimidate me with what we called 'prefects' detention' – say no more! After seeing off Derby in the replay, my form were allowed to stay up late to watch the TV highlights, much to my glee and excitement, while the so-called Derby 'supporters' were disgruntled. The next day, everyone except for me and the head boy were supporting Watford. One of them, Derek, who was a year below me, was a genuine Watford fan and both of us were fierce, but friendly, rivals. One morning, after breakfast and in our dormitory, Derek and I started to argue about who was the better team – Argyle or Watford – and the argument became a war of words, and then a real fist fight followed! Blood sprouted from our punched noses and lips, some splattering on the nearby wall and on our school's cyan shirts. It was a fight that no one who witnessed it could forget. The angry matron reported us to the feared headmaster, who observed both of us bruised, blood-splattered with our egos damaged. Much to our, and to the matron's, surprise, he laughed! He ordered

us to clean up and go to the first lesson of the day. Derek and I shook hands and let the fight be forgotten about, although we both were still fierce-but-friendly rivals up to the semi-final day.

Nick Sturley

The FA Cup run was tremendous. Our victories at West Brom and Derby were superb, and the semi-final against Watford was great. We played really well, and were unlucky on the day.

Peter Hall

Not scoring in the semi-final is my greatest Argyle disappointment. Such a large crowd, just itching to roar in celebration. If we'd scored, I'm sure we would have won, the players would have had such a lift. But the blue touch paper was never lit, and the toast at the end of the day was heroic failure. I was stood next to two Luton fans during the game, who had come to abuse Watford. After the game, taking a few moments just to soak up the last of the atmosphere and watch the crowd begin to melt away (I was at the 'other' end and had an excellent view of the massed ranks on the Holte End), I discovered that one of them had nicked my programme out my coat pocket. Fantastic! On the day, I travelled up alone from Aberystwyth where I was at university. When I emerged into the daylight, a radio reporter saw the scarf came up to me and asked 'Have the boys arrived?' I told him I hadn't come up from Plymouth, whilst thinking of something to tell his microphone. Just as I thought of a quote – 'The only way Watford will be at Wembley is by getting the catering contract' – a bunch of oiks tunelessly chanting 'Argyle' appeared and off he went. All in all, a disappointing day. I saw a few green shirts on the way back, but I just didn't feel like talking to anyone. Something that could have been so very, very good, had been so tantalisingly close. I still feel so disappointed about that.

John Williams

I think I must have had a premonition about this Cup run, because I even went to the Southend away game in the first round. I allowed plenty of time to get there from Plymouth and when I got to Roots Hall, there were only a handful of people there, when out came Leigh Cooper, who gave me a complimentary ticket – the first and only time I ever got in to a match without paying. I really enjoyed the free game and after that round, I was at every match in the run (including the Southend replay), and I think that I still have the ticket stubs to prove it. They say that time is a great healer, but I still believe we were robbed on that day at Villa Park, maybe by bad luck or maybe by the referee, but I do not think we ever really lost the match. We were every bit as good as Watford.

Ken Jones

10 Worst game

Rodney Marsh dived and was awarded a penalty at Home Park on Boxing Day 1967. Everyone was angry – it was never a pen. I think a bus driver (by profession) ran on the pitch to have a swing at the ref. and got himself arrested. At the final whistle, hundreds – maybe thousands – ran on the pitch to get to the ref. We'd lost 1-0 and were struggling at or near the bottom of the League. We went down that season and I still blame Marsh. I ran on the pitch too, that day. It was a muddy pitch and I was wearing, for the very first time, a pair of desert boots given to me for Christmas by my parents, so I could be hip and trendy. They were ruined, Argyle were ruined and so was my Boxing Day evening at home – my dad went ballistic! We signed a defender on loan from Millwall in 1992 called Tony Witter. We played at Bristol Rovers in the FA Cup and lost 5-0. As one of their goals went in, Witter actually laughed. I've never had faith in the loan transfer market since. I hated him for it, so when Trevor Francis clocked Kolinko at Crystal Palace for laughing at an opposing goal, he had my sympathy. The 3-4 Reading game is a bad memory, not least because that evening we were going out to a Christmas Party. I could not get the result out of my mind – I was no fun that night. I can't even start on all the long and lonely trips home from all corners of England (and Wales) when Argyle have under-performed, but a memorable low was when I left the Macclesfield game at Moss Rose in 2000 when we were four down to get home for a dinner engagement that my wife had arranged and I couldn't get out of. So the plan, irrespective of the score, was to head for home (near Bournemouth) at or around half-time. Some bloke shouted down at me as I left 'part-time supporter'. I'd driven there for a little over 45 minutes of football to support my team and then that happened. I didn't know who I wanted to punch: him, the team or myself for having bothered.

Malcolm Sheryn

Remembering your worst moments following Plymouth Argyle leaves you battling forlornly against a tidal wave of memories. My all-time top five worst moments following Argyle, in chronological order, are:

May 1992 – the 1-3 defeat at home to Blackburn which relegated Argyle. I had never experienced relegation before. Peter Shilton had taken over the sick dog in March that year, and had not had much success. Blackburn were on their way upwards with Kenny Dalglish and had to win the final game of the season to make the play-offs. Plymouth needed a win to stay up. David Smith gave Argyle an early lead. But some feeble goalkeeping by Shilton and quick thinking by the thoroughly dislikeable David Speedie decided the affair, as he scored two goals just before half-time. After that, it was a formality: Speedie got a hat-trick. I don't think it had dawned on me that we could really go down until the third one went in. I was inconsolable. The only positive was that it steeled me for disappointments to come.

April 1993 – the 0-3 defeat at home to Exeter on Easter Saturday. Shilton's team of skilful ball players, the well-paid dandies of the old Third Division, were roundly stuffed by the paupers from up the road. Exeter were so fired up, so passionate, and could have won by more. Their performance typified the ethics of manager Alan Ball who was up from the dug-out, shouting and punching the air for most of the game. By contrast, Plymouth's hangdog players and bench didn't fancy a fight, and were a disgrace to the club. McCauley threatened to dock their wages afterwards. If ever you wondered why Chairman Dan felt he had got his fingers (and wallet) burnt by the Shilton years, you only have to remember this match. Shameful. It was the first time I ever booed my own team. Of course, two days later we tonked West Brom 5-2 at the Hawthorns. And that's why football is the greatest game on earth.

May 1994 – the 1-3 defeat in the play-offs against Burnley. We had a great team that season – goals galore, delightful football, fantastic attacking players. We had earned a 0-0 draw at Turf Moor with ten men. No one thought it would be a formality, but when Dwight Marshall scored the opener, a surge of belief and passion swept through the packed old ground. A false dawn if ever there was one. John Francis ripped apart the lightweight, shaky centre-back partnership of Hill and Comyn. The emptiness at the end of the game was palpable. Many of us did not leave the ground for a while. My insides had been wrenched out. I've never been able to express to anyone who wasn't there how it felt. Not just because we lost, but because we had a wonderful side. It was football at it most cruel.

May 1998 – the 1-2 defeat at Burnley, and relegation. We had been poor all season and relegation was no surprise. Yet we travelled to Burnley with hope, and played with a level of belief that would have been helpful several months earlier. Mark Saunders' 25th-minute equaliser was followed by plenty of half-chances. Burnley were not that good either. Earl Jean's late chance in front of the massed Argyle support missed in agonising slow motion. The despair at the end and the thought of an early return to the dregs of Division Three were compounded by the taunting and threats from some of the Burnley fans who had swarmed onto the pitch. They stood in front of us and goaded us. The police and stewards seemed unable to do anything useful. Violence threatened from both sides, and it spilled over in the streets around the ground. The long journey home was not a happy prospect.

April 2000 – the 1-4 defeat away at Macclesfield. Recurring themes of following Plymouth in recent memory include long wasted journeys to tiny, former non-League grounds; gutless, clueless performances from players who seemed only to have met that morning before the match; an apparent absence of any tactical know-how; and no heart or pride in the face of defeat. All these things came together at Macclesfield. I've rarely been one to boo my team off the field. I did that day. I have never left a game before the end. I came mighty close. One of my friends turned on his heels and stormed out in disgust after 30 minutes, when the third one went in. The least a supporter expects from their team is some heart and commitment and effort. You can bear a defeat if you have that. Not for the first or last time, that particular Plymouth team showed none of these qualities. I came away seriously questioning what I was doing following this bunch around the country. I should have waited outside the players' entrance afterwards and demanded my money back from every one of those no-good losers. It still boils my blood to this day.

Toby Jones

Unsurprisingly, Burnley (away) when a point in the final game of the season would have preserved our status. The result was (almost) bearable – what was not (and took an incredible level of self-restraint) was the inability of the local police force to retain Burnley fans behind the fencing and the fact that they tolerated them openly taunting the Argyle fans from the edge of the pitch. And the law did absolutely nothing – despite there having been numerous announcements during the fixture that anyone entering the field of play would be arrested. One was also aware that there was a large contingent of Blackburn fans in the 'Argyle' end, and

they were just itching for the Argyle fans to react – at which they would have been in amongst the Burnley rabble at the drop of a hat. To our credit, not one Argyle fan encroached and the riot possibility was defused. It seems that Burnley are one of the least loved, least respected and most easily detested teams in the League. On that day, it wasn't difficult to realise why.

Bob Gelder

Argyle's first-ever visit to Cheltenham, where we lost 2-0 on 23 November 1999. The most satisfying aspect of the evening was finding a parking space near the Whaddon Road ground. I was so surprised about it that I drove off and returned to it, just to make sure I wasn't dreaming. Then the nightmare started. Radio 5 had reported the evening's weather to be cloudy, breezy, yet dry. Thus my umbrella remained in the car and, of course, it drizzled during the game. And my daughter Lucy cannot allow her parting to get wet. Doubtless, the brolly tip would have been unscrewed and confiscated by a steward anyway. Indeed, the white plastic top of my son's small bottle of lemonade was confiscated, so I hid the aerial of my mobile phone down my sock in case a steward acquired that as a prized trophy. We queued outside one set of turnstiles, patiently, at around 6.25 p.m. Word spread that there was a problem: the gate wouldn't open, the turnstiles were inoperable, or some such hitch. Maybe the club had realised that there would be too many visiting fans for the 1,012 terrace limit. No one told us anything. Police chatted, but no one moved us. I chatted to a really pleasant family from Liskeard with a terri-

Kenny Dalglish steers Blackburn to promotion, relegating Argyle to Division Two in the process.

ble secret: the man was hiding a pasty in his black travel bag. Sinister, I thought. After 15 minutes or so, in memorable primary school country-dancing style, the front of the queue made a cast-off turn to the right. A nifty move. But as we marked time ready to join the cascade, many other Argyle fans from further down the queue in Whaddon Road simply ignored the manoeuvre and headed for the new turnstile destination round the corner. Heck, didn't they know the steps? We joined a bulging queue some five or six people wide, and those at the front were chanting.

We were standing at the gate of an isolated bungalow and, quite obviously, the sounds were echoing off a garage door. Jamie, my 8-year-old son thus asked why Argyle fans were singing in someone's garage. A further wait of 15 minutes led to queues massing well back into Whaddon Road again. We were all in good humour and yet it seemed inevitable that the kick-off would be delayed. It was. The turnstile was opened, but before we could negotiate that, a row of bottle-cap collectors mugged us. The guy with the questionable pasty began to perspire, so I bailed him out by telling a rotund Gloucestershire policeman that this chap was intending to throw an automatic repeating pasty onto the pitch as a racial statement. The PC seemed bemused, yet amazingly allowed the pasty and its owner to pass. Having evaded the stewards' frisking, and feeling inexplicably pleased that we had smuggled my daughter's shoulder-bag toggles through enemy lines, we were then held up by a ludicrous system at the turnstile. Two men scurried to give us tickets, quite unnecessarily delaying access to the stadium further. We then found ourselves on a concourse behind a length of covered enclosure terracing. Parallel rows of uniformed constabulary lined the prescribed route and we negotiated it. It was like country dancing again, promenading this time. We were beginning to realise that we

had been delegated the usual home terrace to view the game from, hence the fierce onlooking law-persons. Toilets. Yes, we could certainly use those. No, we couldn't. Guarded by police, we were told that the loos were out of order, but more were positioned on our terrace. These turned out to be portable toilets. Two singles, maybe for women, one single and the epic 'Toilet Tardis' for men. Designed on the outside to cunningly conceal the fact that well over 1,500 men could urinate inside at the same time, it took up only as much space as a police telephone kiosk. I began thinking about Kidderminster Harriers' ground. Don't know why. No comparison. The referee, Mike Read, appeared to be present at the game in a physical sense only, yet still most of the Argyle fans kept their good humour.

Nightmare at Elm Park, as Argyle throw away a 3-1 lead to lose 4-3.

Despite the performance, the wind-blown drizzle, the puzzling interpretations by the officials and the threat of long journeys home, many Argyle fans kept their spirits up. Amazingly, the public address announcer, maybe a closet Grecian, asked us for MORE patience by staying in the ground until the Cheltenham supporters had dispersed. This was not credible to us. Basically, there was one exit to be used, at the far end of the ground – surely, along with the inadequate toilet facilities, this was a breach of health and safety regulations? The good humour was waning visibly as a smoke bomb was thrown onto the pitch. Or was it my earlier acquaintance's sinister pasty? Whatever, it caused a scuffle with police and stewards and at least one Argyle fan was ejected. He may have considered himself fortunate, because the rest of us were held on our terrace for 15 dreadful minutes and tempers were sorely tested. One small group began to bounce like Tiggers with no costumes, but the police must have discounted it as a dance from the West Country and no action was taken. Eventually, we filed out – beaten, damp, and cold. Most were facing a long ride home. Lucy's parting was ruined. Shoddy treatment for ordinary fans and I can only praise the vast majority of them. Interesting then, that the *Gloucestershire Echo* reported on the Robins' 'stunning display' and one headline announced 'Police Tackle Football Yobs' and spoke of officers escorting a Plymouth hooligan gang called The Central Element out of the county. Yet no apologies for the inconvenience suffered by the real fans, or of Cheltenham Town's poor management of the evening. It was enough to make me want to throw a plastic bottle top at Town's mascot – presumably a Christmas robin, but actually resembling a trussed turkey.

Pete Ray

There are many competitors for worst match. There was the sheer disappointment of seeing Argyle 3-1 up against Reading with twenty minutes to go, and then losing 4-3 in the 1985/86 promotion season when Reading were undefeated at home – mind you, that was a good game of football. For embarrassment, I would pick the last match of the 1974/75 promotion season at Peterborough. I was teaching in Coventry at the time, and I had taken a couple of lads from school to see a 'real' football match. Argyle were already promoted, but needed to win to have an outside chance of the Championship. We duly lost a poor game and some supporters let the team down with truly awful behaviour. I left the ground with a very red face.

Kevin Howarth

The most frustrated, and saddened, I've ever been as an Argyle fan was when we lost 3-0 at Scarborough in May 1999 to seal another season in Division Three. Our team showed no passion, no desire. Sometimes you don't mind a lack of skill, if the effort is there, but that game summed up everything about that side.

Sam Fleet

11 Wembley memories

It was a great day. It was historic and it is unforgettable, and the scenes after the game were fantastic. However, it wasn't that straightforward. Many people eulogise that day as an unfettered party success, as if Plymouth's marvellous support made us a shoo-in for the victory. Hindsight has built a 'day of destiny' aura around the occasion. I remember it differently. I couldn't entirely enjoy the build-up to the game, or indeed, much of the game itself. The whole day was too important. All I was interested in was getting out of the lousy bottom division. We had spent our first ever season down there, and didn't want to go back. Ever. Combine this with years of disappointment and heartbreak when supporting Argyle, and it added up to a day of tension and suffocation and eventual relief. I could not get in to the carnival atmosphere, the face painting revelry and 'big day out' mentality that perhaps typified the younger supporters or those who could detach themselves from the club more easily. I wished I could at the time, but I was stuck with it. Yes, Plymouth had overwhelming support. And yes, we had a manager who was the master of the play-offs. This all added to the weight of expectation, which is not necessarily a good thing. Plus, I had seen the play-off semi-final against Colchester, and the final was never going to top the

second leg at Home Park. Add to this the fact that Darlington were a good side: a better footballing side than Plymouth without a doubt. They had beaten us home and away during the season. Before kick-off, I looked out over a sea of green swathing the Wembley stands, a magnificent sight. I almost felt sorry for the hopelessly outnumbered Darlington supporters. You just thought 'Surely they can't let down support like this'. The build-up seemed to take an age. I just wanted to get on with it. The most striking thing about the afternoon was how uneventful the match was, at least compared to what you expect for such an all-or-nothing game. I'm sure this is partly a compliment to the Plymouth team, because it prevented Darlington from finding a rhythm, and placed more significance on organisation, set pieces and mental strength, rather than flair or individual brilliance. If you watch the highlights, not much of note happened. A few key moments turned the game. Matt Appleby's missed chance in the first half was the height of Darlington's threat. Ronnie Maugé's set-piece header won it. Usually, after Argyle take a lead, you never feel safe. Inexplicably, on that day, I felt more comfortable than normal. The players seemed to believe it was theirs and would not let go. Darlington never really threatened in the latter stages. None of this is to say that the emotions at the end were not wonderful. Relief was the overriding one for me. This turned to joy and only then could I drink in the occasion. Having my dad there with me was probably the best thing about the day. It was fantastic to join the 30,000-odd Argyle fans singing and dancing and celebrating for long after the final whistle. The match had been tortuous, and now we could relax. Of course, the total irony of being rewarded with Wembley glory for not being good enough to win automatic promotion was not lost on us. But we were out of the basement division and destined for better times. Hindsight should not cloud that sentiment either.

Toby Jones

My fondest memory of 'Wemberlee' is the lump in my throat as I absorbed the noise and passion of the singing at the end. OK, they were naff songs – 'Simply the Best' and 'Rockin' All Over the World' – but 'We are the Champions' being sung by 35,000 Argyle fans was inspiring and it will live long in my memory. I always said that I'd never go to see a game at Wembley unless Argyle were there ... that was a special day for me. It's a pity that 60 per cent of the people there on that day will not go again until we're in the Premiership.

Andy Laidlaw

As an ordinary fan I had to decide the best way to get to Wembley – coach, car, plane or train? Another problem was that my daughter Lucy (aged ten) was going to Belgium with her school that Saturday, leaving at 6.30 a.m. Oh, and another problem was I had booked a holiday (!) with the family, starting that Saturday at lunch-time. Persuading my wife to postpone the caravan holiday till the Sunday easily solved that. Fortunately, the train was due to leave at 6.51 a.m., allowing time to see Lucy off. I booked four seats: for me, my son Oliver, my friend Keith Jones and his son Lloyd. Packed up with sandwiches and flask, we met at the station and boarded the train for our special day decked out in green scarves, Oliver with his green wig. What an atmosphere, the train was full of supporters! But what would happen if we lost? How would we cope? We decided to forget that and enjoy the day. We arrived at Paddington, caught the tube and arrived at Wembley two hours before kick-off. I had arranged to meet Tommy Tynan at the ground at 1.30 p.m. as he had travelled down from Sheffield, and was doing some commentary for Westcountry TV. I met Tommy and pointed him in the direction of the television crews. It was good to meet up with him again, and we arranged to meet after the game. We watched all the coaches arrive, all the gold and silver packages taken up by the supporters. We just savoured the atmosphere, fantastic, but where were all the Darlington supporters? We outnumbered them three to one – we deserved to win, didn't we? Only time would tell. We found our seats, opposite the Royal Box – we could see the Argyle directors in the distance, how privileged they were, but we too were privileged being at Wembley with our beloved team. What a tense game, Darlington could have scored but we held out, and then came the magic moment of Ronnie Maugé's goal.

Ronnie scores 'that' goal.

We sang ourselves hoarse right till the final whistle. The loudspeaker sounded out 'We are the Champions' and we all believed it, we had won and were back up to Division Two, thanks to Neil Warnock. We saw Dan in his funny hat jigging on the pitch, relegation had been forgotten, so we enjoyed the moment. We were about the last to leave the stadium, savouring every second. We met with Tommy and looked for a pub, eventually finding a burger bar with a bar licence. After one quick drink, Tommy made his way back to Kings Cross and we left for to Paddington. What a day

– it was more than ninety minutes, it was Argyle at Wembley for the only time in our history and we were there. We sang all the way home on the train, everyone was really happy. Here's to Division Two and progress up the League, or so we thought ...

Paul Stapleton

The Wembley game was the highlight of my 'watching Argyle' life. However, you may be surprised to know that I did not enjoy the game one little bit. Sure, getting to Wembley and the result was fantastic, but the actual match was torture, as the tension was almost breath-stopping. But the celebrations afterwards will always be in my memory. I never want to go through that tension again. Having said that – what will I do IF we get to the play-offs again? Let's be honest, I would be over the moon, but I don't think it would be so bad this time around.

Ken Jones

The greatest day of my football life, except the view was crap, and we were so far up in the stand, we couldn't see the lads collecting the cup from the VIP box! I play the video every so often, when I'm pissed off. I enjoyed the train back up to Watford to pick up the car, as there were several gloomy Darlo fans that definitely needed a pasty and a pint of Plymouth Breweries bitter!

Phil Ramsay

Wembley – what a day. My abiding memory is being inside the ground, looking out of the left Twin Tower and seeing a sudden surge of about 8,000 Argyle fans walking up Wembley Way – about three trains full of fans. Hell of an image.

Andrew Holland

I took my 7-year-old grandson to the Wembley game and I think he enjoyed it. The after-match scenes were something to behold, with Dan McCauley dancing around the pitch wearing Pilgrim Pete's top hat!

Norman Adams

Apart from the game, one memory that sticks in my mind was paying a bloke a pound to become a day member of this social club down one of the back streets. After about an hour, the club was jam-packed. I mentioned to the barman what a great idea it was having this bloke outside, as there were about 300 people now inside. He informed me that they didn't have anyone collecting money, as it was open to anyone on match days. A very easy £300 for that man!

Warren 'Wozzer' Bowden

A fantastic day, though never the greatest of matches, as I think we'd used up all our flair football in the semi-final against Colchester. I guess it's every football fan's dream to see their team win at Wembley though, so to be able to say that I have done that is great. I missed out on the celebrations and civic reception the following day, however, as my brother Martin and I were running the Plymouth Half-Marathon instead. My first ever attempt at the 13 miles, and it was probably adrenalin left over from the previous day that carried me round!

Jim Brock

We had three generations of family members there – my dad, my nephew and me. Dad got a bit fed up with people standing up at key moments and was totally bemused by the singing on the chairs afterwards. He was perplexed by all the fuss about scraping out of the bottom division (the Fourth, as he demeaningly called it). It was my nephew's first real experience of Argyle 'glory' – although he had played on the hallowed turf for the supporters' club team that reached the division supporters' final at the play-offs the year before. Sadly, Dad passed on before the next promotion season, but we're all sort of still together as bricks in Pilgrim Way.

Keith Whitfield

It was hot, it was green and it was nerve-wracking. It was just what football is all about – fantastic.

Timothy Smart

Singing 'Father Abraham' outside a pub in the West End, dancing in the fountain in Trafalgar Square and just being there.

Sue Lawrence

Strangely, memories are brief ... Watching the team coaches arrive, and wondering where the Darlo fans were as everything was green and white. Realising that the great dump hadn't had a facelift since I'd last gone about 15 years before. I realised this as I watched the river of urine running out through the toilet door and under the feet of those in the queue for hot dogs! True. I can't remember much about the game except the goal, then waiting what

seemed like a century for the final whistle afterwards and a feeling of dread each time Appleby got the ball. The great sense of relief at the end, and the realisation that, for once, we'd got the rub of the green. Seeing Noddy at full volume heading for the tube after the final whistle. Getting back in my car to drive back up to Newcastle, with scarf out of window, only to see coach-loads of miserable faces doing hand gestures at me. It's a long way back up the A1! Listening to *606*, expecting a show dedicated to our day, and not hearing one call on air from an Argyle fan, and only the briefest of mentions that we'd even played! Still, a fine day, but not half as good as doing it properly in 2001/02!

Chris Ramsay

It was part of a very crazy weekend. I travelled to the game with two Darlington fans, and attempted to have a drink at The Globe near Baker Street, but all the windows had been put out minutes before. I was still a bit in the clouds from the previous night's activities, but the game was quite dull and I found playing 'Simply the Best' extremely poor, considering both teams finished outside the top three. Travelling back to Catterick, not much needed to be said in the car, except when I requested my tape to be played, which happened to be a recording on a walkman of the crowd. They weren't happy at all! A couple more days enjoying the finer things in life nearly killed one Darlo fan, who collapsed with exhaustion on the Monday – top weekend!

Neil Carhart

Wembley 1996 – many thought that this was the greatest day in the club's history. I beg to differ. Yes, it was great to see my team play at the most famous stadium in the world, but it was as a result of finishing fourth in the League! It was a great day out for many – mostly the 30,000 hangers-on. The 5,000 'true' Argyle fans couldn't really enjoy the occasion until it was over, because they were the ones who cared enough to know what was actually at stake, rather than having a jolly in the 'Smoke'. The match at Wembley was not a great spectacle. We deserved to win – and having finished in fourth place (i.e. one of the proper promotion positions) deserved to go up anyway.

Steve Nicholson

I'd promised my missus that I'd get back to Nottingham sober-ish at a reasonable time and, being the reliable, decent, honest fellow that I am, I managed to catch the train that I'd said I would from St Pancras. I'd split up with my brother, who was heading back to Plymouth, and I made my way to the station where I managed to grab a quick pint in the bar. My only companions were some Saturday shoppers and couple of extremely dejected-looking Darlington fans. Naturally, I was still in a fairly euphoric state and I wanted to share my joy, but none of these struck me as being ideal drinking companions. I offered my condolences to the Darlo lads, who took it all in very good heart and said 'well done' and all that, but I couldn't see

The victorious Argyle team celebrate the play-off final win over Darlington.

myself sharing a can or two with them on the way back as I didn't really want to gloat. I knew exactly how I'd be feeling if the result had gone their way and the last thing I'd have wanted to do was spend a couple of hours on a train with opposition supporters, no matter how gracious in victory they were. So, I spent the next two hours sitting on my own, smoking too much, gagging for a pint, itching to celebrate and talk football. The train arrived at Nottingham on time and Jane was there to meet me. She, as any football widow worth her salt should be, was aware of the score and looked as delighted as someone with no real liking for the game or for Argyle could manage. She was pleased, and somewhat amazed, that I'd managed to get back on time and that I was still sober, and I think that she sensed I was wishing that I was somewhere in the West End in a pub full of Janners, celebrating our victory properly. To her eternal credit, she pointed the car homewards and really put her foot down so I could get to the pub nearest our house in plenty of time to get a few pints down my neck. Despite my liking for the beer, I must say that I don't go out drinking in the village where I live very often, mainly because the place is a dump, so my 'local' is only local in the geographical sense and not in the 'spiritual'

Mick Heathcote lifts the trophy as Argyle ascend to Division Two.

way that a real local is. I've chatted with a few of the lads there about football from time to time and although most of them are plastic Mancs, there are a few real fans – a mixture of Mansfield, Forest and Newcastle mainly, (there are quite a few ex-pat Geordies round here who moved here for the mining when we still had mines) with one or two fans of the two Sheffield clubs thrown in. However, on this night of all nights, there were none to be found – the place was full of lemon-sweatered, Farah slack-wearing gardening freaks out with 'the wife' for the Saturday night ritual. I walked up to the bar, ordered a pint and downed it in one. The landlord said something like 'Blimey, mate, you were thirsty' and Jane informed him that I was celebrating Argyle's famous victory at the 'Theatre Of Dreams'. 'Oh', he said, 'what was the score?' 'One-nil', I beamed. 'Couldn't have been much of a game', he replied. He didn't get it. I drank my second pint and went home.

Neil Jenkins

Glimpsing the Twin Towers and seeing car- and coach-loads of Argyle fans and realising my team were going to play there at last brought tears to my eyes! Milling around in the sun before going into the ground, buying souvenirs, everyone taking photos, everyone grinning from ear to ear. Waiting in the ground before the start and seeing 'Argyle' everywhere and hearing West Country accents, whilst looking out over the hallowed turf! The amazing Argyle support inside the ground. Feeling a little bit sorry for Darlo. The male streaker (makes a change!). Looking up at the scoreboard – 1-0 up. Standing on the seats to sing 'We are the Champions' and 'Rockin' all over the World'. Queuing to leave in the car afterwards, horns blaring, green and white everywhere. Driving back down the M25 to Kent (having left most of the Argyle convoy heading west down M4/M3), my Argyle flag and scarf flapping in the wind and getting amazed and puzzled stares from other drivers. But most of all, being immensely grateful to Warnock, for being able to keep the team focused on the prize of promotion. I have to admit I had to keep reminding myself that was the reason we were there. An amazing day, which I'll never forget!

Sarah Decent

My wife, Janet, was expecting Michael, our fourth child. We were living at Barry, Wales. The midwife came to call and said to me, 'Your wife tells me that you are planning to go to Wembley on Saturday. What will you do if the baby arrives early?' I replied, 'This will be our fourth baby, but Argyle have never been to Wembley before and I am not going to miss it.' Michael was born the following Wednesday.

John Haley

12 Derby games

Exeter City 2 Argyle 3, 2 March 1994. This was a match that will live in the memory for years to come. After all, a first win since 1928 at the home of the Grecians is a notable landmark, and what a season in which to achieve it. This was probably one of the best sides to be clad in the noble green and white since the war, who played football worthy of a higher division (a right to be cruelly denied), in the manner it should be. The match was eagerly awaited by all concerned. In particular, Greens fans believed that revenge for the previous season's inept double humiliation was there for the taking. The evening was clear and a buzz filled the air around Exeter. Being a student at the university, I managed to get a ticket – for the Big Bank. On arriving at the ground, I took my place on the terraces, with envious glances at the Green Army in the away end. To my pleasant surprise, however, a chorus of 'England's number one' (in recognition of the late, great Alan Nicholls' call-up to the England Under-21 squad) rang out from all around me on our hero's arrival at the Big Bank goal. I was not alone. The match commenced and Exeter played above themselves. However, this did not prevent Argyle, without the notable talents of Dalton and Marshall, from gaining a hold on the game. Even Steve McCall managed a shot. Midway through the half, déjà vu returned. A good move from City resulted in a smart back-heel by Mark Cooper to beat Alan and leave the 'Gyles fans shocked. The second half began, and it was not long before a magnificent Mark Patterson scored an equaliser, off a hapless City defender. The Green Army at both ends erupted. Still in a daze at the sudden turn in fortunes, and hardly with a chance to shout 'well done, Patto', a deflection to the edge of the City box was drilled into the bottom corner by Wayne Burnett. 1-2 – we were in front at St. James' Park! The game was now ours, and the players, to their credit, played with a professionalism all too often missing from the men in green (remember Elm Park in 1985). Then, with the clock counting down, Micky 'Trigger' Evans (these were the days when he truly could be described as a striker) smashed the ball into the roof of the City net from close in. Seasons of embarrassment were shed in that one instant, and the Green Army made enough noise to outsing the City faithful. Surely now victory was ours? But, with minutes to go, Adekola grabbed a second for City out of the blue. Green hearts were in mouths. We could not let this slip now, could we? Even though Exeter pushed forward with all their worth, the makeshift Greens defence held firm (Hill had been cynically chopped down by Turner). Eventually, the whistle blew and the carnival began. St James' Park was a mass of green and white. This was a match that saw us not only beat Exeter, but outplay and outclass them on their own ground – a truly satisfying experience, ESPECIALLY for those Argyle fans trapped in Exeter!

Toby Jackson (PASTIE – Plymouth Argyle Supporter Trapped in Exeter)

3-2 to the Argyle, after years of non-success, sitting in the wooden seats. Oh, the euphoric feeling at that long-awaited final whistle which laid the bogey to rest. Subsequently, yet another, more recent, 3-2 victory over Exeter, when Ian Stonebridge rose like a salmon to clinch it with Argyle's third goal in the 89th minute. The Exeter fan alongside me in the Ivor Doble Stand stormed out, saying that we were jammy and that we would lose far more games than we would win that season. We were promoted with a record 102 points! Just goes to show what an Exeter fan knows about football. 'Blakey' left shortly after. It was enlightening, above all else, to hear what he had to say about Buster Phillips. Talk about venting one's

Stoney, Trigger and Buster after the 3-2 away win in the Championship season.

Steve Adams starts the scoring on a memorable night at Home Park, as Argyle hammer the Grecians 3-0.

spleen! Mind you, they then went and bought McCarthorse, complete with two elbows. Says it all, really.

Bob Gelder

Exeter City away, March 1994. The first away victory I saw in a Devon derby came at Exeter on a Tuesday night in March 1994, during our play-off season. The terrace was incredibly cramped. The whole scene must have been a fire hazard, owing to the overwhelming amount of newspaper confetti that we unleashed at the start.

It must have been 3in deep everywhere. I had my right arm in plaster at the time, which made it easier to pick me out in photos and TV highlights. The atmosphere was claustrophobic – it was one of those games where you were too caught up in the tension to pay much heed to the football being played. Argyle struggled in the first half, with Cooper giving Exeter the lead after half-an-hour. It looked to be heading the way of other recent games at St James'. In the second half, Plymouth played good football with plenty of spirit. A surging run by Mark Patterson produced an own goal from the Grecians just after half-time. Then Wayne Burnett scored with a terrific placed shot from the edge of the area after a neat build-up. I was about 10ft away from the ball as it nestled in the corner. It felt like the cliché of the crowd sucking the ball goalwards. A Nugent cross was slammed home at the near post by Evans, and again I was lost in a crush of hysteria behind the goal. Of course, Argyle had to make it painful when Adekola scored for City with less than 10 minutes to go, but we hung on. Torquay United away in March 2000 was another classic – we went to Torquay in the midst of another turgid season and came away having won in some style. But the memories have as much to do with the rest of the day as the

game itself. During the drive down, we had experienced some patchy weather and expected rain. Whilst standing on the small exposed away terrace, I could see ominous black clouds approaching from our right. The teams warmed up in pleasant conditions. Literally, as the referee whistled to start the match, the heavens opened. It didn't just rain. It hailed. It hailed a fast, piercing freak storm. Most people were not dressed to cope with this, in t-shirts and thin jackets. The hailstones hurt. You had to protect yourself. Watching the match was secondary to hiding from Nature. You could barely see beyond the halfway line. Then after about 20 minutes, it stopped, and the sun came out.

Sean McCarthy arrives and then departs within minutes on his return to Home Park.

Gradually, we all thawed and dried out. The game came to life as well. The mercurial (definition: has great skill which is only occasionally used, doesn't like to tackle back, has unkempt hairstyle, mostly found in the 1970s – see Worthington, Frank) Paul McGregor had one of his imperious days. He played at a level above the others on the pitch, and he knew it. McGregor's third goal, and Argyle's fourth, after 78 minutes was the height of bravado. He found himself through one-on-one with the 'keeper. He took his time, drew the goalie, and then slotted the ball through his legs as if it were easier than breathing. He didn't run around or celebrate, he just stood there and gloated, which is exactly what we were feeling on the terraces at that moment. Wonderful stuff. My other top memory will win no prizes for originality – Exeter City at home, February 2002. Argyle soundly thumped Exeter on a Tuesday night on their way to the Division Three title. The gulf in class, in resources, and in (whisper it quietly) potential was as stark as it has ever been that night. In front of the biggest Division Three crowd to that date of 16,369 in Plymouth's shiny new stadium, Exeter were out-thought, out-fought and out-played. The whole occasion demonstrated why I always find it hard to become as vitriolic as some fans do about City. City arrived on the back of some impressive away form. They had made a habit of coming to Home Park and showing a greater desire than Argyle in recent times. The 3-0 scoreline, and more so the performance, showed how much

David Friio scores in another Donkey Derby win.

Chris Hargreaves plays through the hailstorm as Argyle crush Torquay with a McGregor hat-trick.

the Greens had changed under Paul Sturrock. Argyle took a 5th-minute lead with a scrappy Steve Adams goal after Keystone Cop defending from City. Marino Keith doubled the lead with a deflected header. The goals had an element of fortune, but the all-round display was captivating. Exeter barely threatened. We all thought Keith had crowned the evening with his sublime long-range lob for number three on 74 minutes, but the cherry on the icing on the cake was yet to come. Sean McCarthy had come off the Exeter bench after 69 minutes. A figure of ridicule and fun in recent years, he was shown no mercy in the time-honoured style of football fans everywhere. For me, he represented the overpaid, under-cooked, uninspiring Plymouth of the late Nineties: a player who spent too much of his time fouling, falling over, being suspended and providing regular comedy interludes, not to mention being paid a pretty penny to do so. So Sean lumbered on to jeers and was all arse and elbows for just under 10 minutes. He then became involved in a bit of strong-arm tussling with Graham Coughlan. McCarthy instinctively threw an elbow into Coughlan's face, with the referee standing but a few yards away. The cheers that greeted his red card and amble to the dressing room were

The crowd at Plainmoor, after the hailstorm had passed.

nearly as big as for the third goal. I almost, almost felt sorry for Sean. But football is cruel, and our evening of joy was complete.

Toby Jones

Well, the Exeter City part is easy to answer, because I enjoy any match that we win against them, especially away. But, let's be honest, we have not won that many away – mainly, I think, because a succession of managers did not feel that it was worth sending more than the reserve side to tackle a Fourth Division club. However, to answer the question, without any doubt the game that I shall forever remember was played on 2 December 2000 and we won 0-2. It was David Friio's first game for Argyle, I was there and I have the t-shirt to prove it. Torquay? Well, without any doubt, my match to remember was the battle of Boxing Day 1969, when Torquay were near the top of the Third Division, having won 11 games on the trot, and Argyle had been struggling to put anything together. Argyle's manager, Billy Bingham, promised the fans that we would only lose over his dead body, and so, on the day, the Torquay fans brought a full-sized coffin and paraded it around the ground before the game. I had a horrible feeling that Billy was going to have to eat his words. The game kicked off in front of about an 18,000-strong crowd but, by the final whistle, this was considerably down, as the Torquay fans had nearly all gone home. Argyle were leading 6-0 with Norman Piper, who had controlled the match, getting two (one a penalty) and the mighty Mike Bickle getting four. What else can I say?

Ken Jones

Most of my memories of Exeter are bad ones. We never played them in my early days as an Argyle fan – possibly another reason why I don't 'hate' them. Our paths first crossed in the late Seventies, but the first match that springs to mind was on Boxing Day in 1980. We had loads of family down that Christmas, and I convinced them all that an afternoon at Home Park watching Argyle thrash their local rivals would be great entertainment. We were awful and lost 2-0, much to my per-

sonal embarrassment. Because of their relegation and our promotion, we didn't play them again for a few years. In 1993/94, I missed our first win at St James Park since the Twenties because of work, but, of course, I was there to witness two awful displays the following season, when they beat us 2-0 at their place on Boxing Day and 3-0 at Home Park. On both occasions, we were lucky to get nil. My happiest Exeter memory was actually as recent as 2002. I never liked Sean McCarthy as a player. When he first left Argyle, he was pretty uncomplimentary about the club, so I was dead against his return. He was useless for two seasons and only started trying when he needed to earn a new contract. Having failed to convince Sturrock to give him one, he joined Exeter and was sub. for the match at Home Park. He was brought on to try to retrieve the game for them, but was sent off within 10 minutes of being on the field. How sweet was that? The cheers for him leaving the field were as loud as the boos when he came on.

Steve Nicholson

The magnificent Nou Home Park.